> FULLY REVISED AND UPDATED

Bicycling MAGAZINE'S

Skills and Techniques to Master Any Terrain

MOUNTAIN BIKING SKILLS

EDITED BY BEN HEWITT

RODALE

© 2005 by Rodale Inc.

Cover photograph by Bill Hatcher/Getty Images
Interior photographs by Bigshots/Getty Images (page 12); Jakob Helbig/Getty Images (page 41); Chase Jarvis/Getty Images (page 33); John Kelly/Getty Images (pages 29 and 86); Darryl Lenuik/Getty Images (page 26); David Madison/Getty Images (page 106); Photodisc Collection/Getty Images (page 88); Plush Studios/Getty Images (page 79); Richard Price/Getty Images (page 15); and Barry Tessman/Getty Images (page 22)
Interior illustration by Daniel Vasconcellos
"Mountain Biking Position," starting on page 109, is adapted from *Mountain Bike Like a Champion* by Ned Overend with Ed Pavelka.

Portions of this book were originally published as *Bicycling® Magazine's Mountain Biking Skills* by Rodale Inc. © 2000.

Book design by Drew Frantzen

Library of Congress Cataloging-in-Publication Data
Bicycling magazine's mountain biking skills : skills and techniques to master any terrain / edited by Ben Hewitt.— Fully rev. and updated.
p.   cm.
Includes index.
ISBN-13 978–1–59486–299–1 paperback
ISBN-10 1–59486–299–0 paperback
1. All terrain cycling.   I. Hewitt, Ben, date.   II. Bicycling.   III. Title: Mountain biking skills.
GV1056.B55   2005
796.6'3—dc22   2005023045

Distributed to the trade by Holtzbrinck Publishers

2   4   6   8   10   9   7   5   3   paperback

RODALE
LIVE YOUR WHOLE LIFE™

We inspire and enable people to improve their lives and the world around them
For more of our products visit **rodalestore.com** or call 800-848-4735

CONTENTS

INTRODUCTION

Few sports have enjoyed as meteoric a rise as mountain biking. Consider: Just over a quarter century ago, the mountain biking community was confined to a handful of pioneering cyclists in northern California. They favored shoulder-length hair held back by bandanas, flowing beards swept back by the breeze (on the men, at least), and bellbottom jeans that flapped and popped as they rocketed modified beach cruisers down the fire roads of the state's coastal peaks. They were a motley lot, but from the smiles carved into their mud-flecked cheeks, one thing was clear: It wouldn't be long before the mountain biking phenomenon spread.

It wasn't. In 1981, Specialized introduced its Stumpjumper mountain bike, the first mass-produced bicycle designed specifically for off-road riding. It boasted 15 gears (modern mountain bikes have as many as 27), and a hodgepodge of components borrowed from touring and road models. It was a resounding success, and within months, the sport had spread like a virus across America and into neighboring countries. By the mid-'80s, dozens of manufacturers had added mountain bikes to their product lines, and the term "mountain biking" had earned a place in cycling history.

And that was just the beginning. Before another decade passed, mountain biking would be an Olympic sport, and it was inextricably linked with the marketing of "extreme." Bellbottoms and bandanas had been replaced by lycra cycling shorts and helmets, and the bikes themselves were hardly recognizable: Front-suspension forks had become nearly ubiquitous, and manufacturers were experimenting with exotic frame materials like carbon fiber and titanium. About the only things that remained unchanged were the mud and grins.

That's still true today, though the sport continues to evolve in ways its founders could never have foreseen. These days, it's not uncommon to see young (and a few old!) mountain bikers launch themselves off 10- and even 20-foot drops, utilizing every last centimeter of their bike's suspension travel. The sport of "freeriding," a mountain biking subset that typically involves fast descents, big jumps, and man-made stunts like ladder bridges and teeter-totters, has captured the imaginations of young riders. Manufacturers have responded by building heavy-duty bikes with as much as 8 inches of suspension travel, disc brakes, and tires nearly as wide as those found on motor-powered dirt bikes. Meanwhile, hundreds of thousands of riders still gather at trailheads every week, seeking the same sense of freedom and adventure that drew the sport's first participants into the mountains nearly 3 decades ago.

If you're reading this book, then you're on the same quest. Consider this book your (off) road map. On these pages, you'll find straight talk and hot tips from some of the sport's biggest stars and—just as important—from people like you, regular folk who spend every free minute riding (or thinking about riding) their mountain bikes. Listen carefully to what they have to say: You're about to join their ranks.

As you read through these pages, remember: There are no hard-and-fast rules to mountain biking. The information gathered here will certainly help you become a more proficient off-road cyclist. But if ever it feels like information overload, relax. Mark your page, put the book down, and go ride. That's what it's all about.

1 >>>

DIRT FOR ROADIES (AND EVERYONE ELSE)

When **Bob Roll** was a pro road racer, he covered thousands of miles in the Tour de France and European classics like Paris Roubaix, racing elbow-to-elbow in 150-man pelotons at 35 mph on roads so rough you'd cringe just driving a car over them. His worst injury? Irritating road rash.

In the early '90s, Roll traded his road bike for a mountain bike. In his first race, he almost died. The event was the now-defunct Cactus Cup; Roll crashed on a tricky piece of desert singletrack, in the process gouging a hole in his arm, which released a geyser of blood from an artery. A doctor in the medical tent patched him up, but it was a less than auspicious start to mountain biking for one of America's most experienced road racers.

Roll survived many more years of off-road racing without grievous injury. Now retired from competition, he serves as on-air commentator to the Outdoor Life Network, lending his unique perspective and outrageous sense of humor to the network's cycling coverage. On the following pages, he lends us his four cardinal rules for a successful (read: hospital-free) transition from pavement to the wild, wooly world of mountain biking. Even if you don't have a road riding background, these tips will help you get hooked on the knobby hobby.

Rule 1: Find Your Inner Child

Kids taught me plenty. It's their capacity for learning, their lack of self-consciousness, their delight in wild abandon that makes them so relaxed and natural on their bikes. So I changed my attitude and became a kid again, reveling in the process of learning. This attitude adjustment is the first step to loving dirt.

Rule 2: Pay Attention to Traction

On the road, traction isn't a big issue. You either have it or you don't. But on dirt, not only can your tires skid, the ground itself may move under your wheels. Maintaining traction (and staying confident when you lose it) is the most difficult adjustment in making the transition from road to singletrack.

First, relax. Terror leads to a death grip on the handlebar. Picture a firm, friendly handshake—you don't want to be a dead fish, but you're not out to crush the other person's hand, either. Even more important is the cushioning effect of your limbs. Modern bikes provide 3 to 6 inches of suspension—but arms and legs are good for several feet of cush. A roadie can afford to be as stiff as a Supreme Court justice, but a mountain biker has to loosen up. Think Bob Marley, not John Philip Sousa.

To improve climbing traction on steep, loose surfaces, scoot forward on your saddle to keep enough weight on the front wheel so it doesn't wander off your chosen line. If you put too much weight forward, the rear wheel will spin, so bend at the waist to distribute your weight evenly. Push your heels down with each pedal stroke and concentrate on a smooth spin because jerky pedaling can cause the rear wheel to break loose. Wrap your thumbs under the bar and pull back in time with your downstroke to weight the rear tire.

For better descending traction, keep the pedals horizontal. Rise slightly off the saddle and move your weight to the rear so that you don't go over the bar if you get knocked offline or bash your front wheel into a rock. On steep descents, move behind the saddle. If you're going in a straight line, use both front and rear brakes. But as soon as you change direction, ease off the front stopper or the wheel may wash out unexpectedly.

Rule 3: Learn to Balance

On a road bike, your point of balance is dependent on two positions: sitting or standing. But on technical terrain, you're all over a mountain bike, scrunching forward on steep climbs, standing briefly to absorb shocks from rough trails, letting your butt hang off the back of the saddle on rubbly downhill chutes.

To improve balance, relax your arms and legs. (There's that word again. Got it?) If you're stiff-armed on a road climb, your steering won't be affected much—but if you try it on a singletrack ascent, your front wheel will weave all over. On descents, center your torso between the handlebar and seat, with your belly button as your center of gravity. Let the bike move under you while your arms and legs absorb and deflect hits from the trail.

Rule 4: Keep Your Eye on the Good Line

Off-road, "poor vision" doesn't mean you need glasses. Instead, it refers to the common habit of fixing your sight on what you fear (that big rock in the middle of the trail, for instance). Before you know it, your motor skills follow your line of sight and you smash into the very hazard you wanted to avoid.

Register the location of obstacles and dangers peripherally. Continually scan the trail both directly ahead of your front tire and 15 to 30 feet farther along. Good vision allows you to read the trail and anticipate problems, thus avoiding near-death experiences.

DE-TECHING THE TECH

Technologically speaking, mountain biking used to be a pretty simple affair. Early mountain bikes were cobbled together out of parts hijacked from road, touring, and beach cruiser models. Throughout the '80s, manufacturers slowly turned up the tech quotient, but for the most part, the goal was to create simple, durable machines that wouldn't leave their masters stranded deep in the backcountry.

Then came the '90s, and with them, the advent of suspension (actually, the first mass-produced suspension fork, Rock Shox's RS-1, was introduced in '89, but that's close enough). Hard-charging downhill riders embraced suspension, along with the greater control, speed, and comfort it provided. Pundits scoffed, claiming that the increased complexity, weight, and cost were hardly worth the benefits. Wondering who won that argument? Walk into any bike shop in North America (heck, in the world), and you'll have your answer. Today, almost every true mountain bike on the market is equipped with front suspension, and increasingly, bikes equipped with front and rear suspension are taking over. And motorcycle-like disc brakes, many operated via hydraulic fluid, are quickly gaining popularity for their increased stopping power, particularly in inclement weather.

The progress has been remarkable. While it's true that early suspension designs were plagued by reliability problems and excessive weight, modern shocks (both front and rear) are models of reliability and customization, allowing riders to "tune" their suspension to suit their size, riding style, and terrain of choice. Still, the generic term "mountain bike" is just that: generic. To fully appreciate and understand the state of mountain bike technology, it's critical to examine all its genres.

Cross-Country Hardtail

Think of this as the classic mountain bike. Of course, "classic" also rings of "outdated," and for most riders, that's exactly what the cross-country hardtail is. "Hardtail" refers to the fact that these bikes lack rear suspension, though they're almost ubiquitously equipped with front-suspension forks offering between 3 and 4 inches of travel.

Sweet: Light (20–25 pounds); relatively inexpensive; faster than full-suspension bikes over smooth terrain

Beat: Slower, less comfortable, and less control over rough terrain compared to full-suspension designs

Buy one if: You're a shave-your-legs serious cross-country racer or don't actually ride off-road all that much

Cross-Country Full-Suspension

Recent advances in shock technology have made these bikes—which feature 3 to 4 inches of travel front and rear—pedal with near hardtail efficiency on climbs and smooth terrain, while still taking the bite out of bumpy trails. A cross-country full-suspension bike will be faster than a hardtail over all but the tamest of trails, while offering greater control and comfort and decreasing fatigue on long rides. Spend enough coin, and you can get a cross-country full-suspension bike that weighs less than 25 pounds.

Sweet: Relatively light; greater control and comfort than a hardtail

Beat: Pricier and slightly heavier than a hardtail; doesn't offer enough suspension travel for fast riding over rough terrain

Buy one if: You cherish speed above all else

All-Mountain Full-Suspension

This category, which is brimming with 26- to 32-pound bikes boasting 4 to 6 inches of front and rear travel and equipped with disc brakes, represents the middle ground of modern mountain biking. In other words, if you're looking for a bike to simply ride up hills and down, short rides and long, this is your bike. It's a jack-of-all-trades sort of steed, for jack-of-all-trades sorts of riders. Not surprisingly, then, all-mountain full-suspension bikes now comprise the bulk of the market, making it a fairly straightforward procedure to find a model that fits your personality and budget.

Sweet: Does pretty much everything well; still fairly light and efficient while climbing and over smooth terrain

Beat: Jack-of-all-trades, sure, but master of none; inexpensive models can be heavy

Buy one if: You get sweaty palms just looking at a topo map

All-Mountain and Jumping Hardtail

Featuring thick-tubed frames built to take ungodly levels of abuse, these bikes are designed for riders who demand the durability and precision that only a hardtail can deliver. These are true specialty bikes, suitable for the rare breed of rider who thinks nothing of catching a dozen feet of air and has a body young and supple enough to take the punishment upon landing.

Sweet: Pretty much unbreakable; relatively cheap

Beat: Overbuilt hardtail frames are a kick in the ass—literally—over rough terrain

Buy one if: You've already had a few mountain bikes—and broken them all

Freeride

To discuss freeride bikes, it's critical to first decide what freeriding is. Some people consider freeriding to be any riding that occurs in an unstructured environment; others associate it with ambulance-baiting stunts and descents down steep mountain faces. Indeed, it's the latter definition that's captured the attention of the mainstream media, and it's that definition manufacturers use when designing and building these portly steeds, which feature as much as 9 inches of suspension travel, disc brakes with massive 8-inch rotors, and knobby tires so wide they wouldn't look out of place on a motorized dirt bike.

Sweet: In the right situation (namely, pointed downhill over nasty jumps and drops), freeride bikes come alive and allow their pilot to do things he'd never even dreamed of

Beat: In any other situation, they're heavy (35–40 pounds) and downright slow

Buy one if: You live near a ski resort that offers lift-served mountain biking

Downhill

Frankly, downhill bikes aren't a lot different from their freeride cousins. That's because downhill racing is essentially the same thing as freeriding, only with a stopwatch put to it.

Sweet: Purposely built to take the abuse of throwing oneself down a mountain at warp speed

Beat: Not good for much else, except maybe an expensive boat anchor

Buy one if: Throwing yourself down mountains at warp speed sounds like a fine way to spend your Sundays

3

THE HOUR OF POWER

Albert Einstein declared that time is a continuum and that hours and days and weeks are mortal constructs that have little validity. What did that joker know? He discovered relativity, so he had tenure. That's practically a license to ride whenever you want.

This is for those of you who aren't Einstein, who live regular, stressed-out lives where going for a ride is often the first thing that gets crossed off your to-do list.

Suppose you have just 60 minutes to be a mountain biker. These "hours of power" require tricks you can use in that limited time frame to keep your off-road monkey happy.

First, the principles of a power hour.

It may not be epic. This is about squeezing a lot out of a little. That goes against the whole idea of the major off-road adventure. Save that for the weekend and use these midweek hours to keep up your interest.

It may not be biking. Don't feel bad if you just can't do it. The world sucks sometimes. Just because you can't find even an hour is no reason to feel guilty. Sometimes, it's impossible to ride. That's okay. Your bike will still be there when you're ready to ride. And the time off will only make you hungrier for dirt. "If I miss a few days of riding and find myself feeling irritable and depressed over it, I use that experience to motivate me to get out the door," says Dirk Anderson, an avid rider with a demanding job as an attorney that often has him working 60-hour weeks. "And you know what? That first ride back is always one of the sweetest of the season."

It has to be fun. Never treat biking—for an hour or for any length of time—as just another chore. Down that road lies burnout.

An Evangelical Message

What's that, you say, my friend? "I don't even have an hour. During the week, I work like a dog, and on weekends I have to walk him." Life is difficult, brother. This is a busy world. Part of it is how you look at mountain biking. Despite what was said earlier about not feeling guilty, there is a commitment involved in being a mountain biker. The people who don't burn out, who find the time, are the ones who see the sport as something more than a necessary activity required to stay fit. They view off-roading as a spiritual pursuit; they see the bike as a tool that gets them closer to nature, helps them appreciate solitude, and challenges their physical and mental limits. If you cannot accept the bike in your life, if the two-wheeled chariot is more and more removed from your soul, if the thing you once loved seems to have vanished into a world of obligation, then it's time to rethink your priorities. Love is not a luxury. It is a right.

There's no doubt about it: Mountain biking is hard to do in an hour. You have to change clothes, get to the dirt, ride it, and get back. So the weekday solutions suggested here don't necessarily involve a lot of dirt or a lot of high-speed action. They're just simple ways to get in some pedaling.

Sometimes you just can't do a ride in an hour. So included here are some ideas to help you stay physically ready and psyched to ride. Be warned: Some of them may sound silly.

Work-ing It In

When it comes to riding at work, you have two options: your daily commute and your lunch hour. Now, bike commuting isn't for everybody. It's better to look at it as just one of the options you have for adding some fitness to your workday. Here are some hints.

Get a slow bike. The Dutch ride around on clunky three-speeds for a reason: The low cadence keeps them from working up a sweat. If you don't have showers at work, this is a great thing. Bonus: You can buy a cheap three-speed for next to nothing at a garage sale. Of course, don't try to outrun city buses on one of these rigs. You WILL lose.

Wipe down. If there are no showers available where you work, you can use a washcloth doused with rubbing alcohol. The alcohol cools you enough to stop perspiration and kills odor-causing germs.

One-way it. Commute home only. Drive your bike in on a Wednesday and then ride it home. On Thursday, either ride back to work, thumb a ride, or crawl.

Go to the gym. Besides using the gym for nonbike workouts—locally owned ones that cater to bodybuilders are usually the friendliest, and they often have a couple of underutilized stairclimbers—you might be able to convince the manager to let you pay a few bucks just to shower. Some of these gyms have a day rate.

Do something else. If you have 1 hour and a place to shower, it might be better to go running or inline skating. The storage problem for your bike is solved. Hopefully, none of your biking buddies will see you. If they do, pretend you lost a bet.

Telecommute 1 day a week. If your company has a work-at-home option, see if you can get in on it. And then abuse it by taking a long, off-road lunch.

Just Do One Thing

Many mountain bikers have the idea that every ride has to be awesome, epic, perfect. Don't fall victim to this way of thinking. If all you have is an hour, try to pick just one of those attributes. Here are some ideas for subject-specific jaunts.

Make it a skill session. Concentrate only on learning something you want to do. It may not be possible to get tons of dirt in 60 minutes, but you might be able to ride circles around a parking lot and learn to pop wheelies. Find a ramp and learn to jump. If that sounds dumb to you, think back to when you were a kid. You probably did the same thing for hours.

Make it a fun session. Take a sightseeing trip. Cruise around the park, watching skaters fall down. Don't even worry about riding for the full hour. Just take half that time to go someplace nice for a quick lunch, like to the hot dog stand over by the guy with the tie cart.

Make it a road ride. If sweat and storage aren't issues, you can get a fantastic workout in an hour by doing intervals. This means riding as hard as you can for a short burst (usually a minute or two), then easing back for the same amount of time. Repeat 5 to 10 times. It hurts, but it really is a great way to get fitter and faster. Including the warmup and cooldown, you can do it in 30 to 40 minutes. There'll be time remaining to erase it all with an Extra-Value Meal. Just don't do it every day (the intervals, or the Extra-Value Meal).

Those Times When You Can't Ride

You can't bike all the time.

Sometimes you just have to say, "I'm not gonna ride. I'm gonna . . . hmmm. . . do something else that has to do with my bike!" That should endear you to your loved ones. Here are some hour-long projects to get you started on the road to divorce court.

Tackle a 1-hour tune-up. There's a lot you can do in 60 minutes to make your bike run better. Start by cleaning it. You can even pull the chain and give the drivetrain a real scrub. Then, adjust your gears. Time left? True your wheels. Still have time left? Get a job at the local bike shop. They need quick guys like you.

Try a tune-up alternative. Put your bike in the car. Drive to the bike shop. Drop it off. Go get a massage. Come home. That counts as an hour, and if you repeat the whole thing when you pick the bike up, that's two "bike sessions" in 1 week!

Do a brake job. This is an hour-long project that really will make the time that you do ride better. Start by replacing your brake pads. It's easy to do; most pads come with instructions. That should take you

30 minutes or so. Spend the rest of the time getting the old baked-on pad residue off your rims. Use a piece of fine steel wool. You'll be amazed at the difference. Don't use steel wool if you have ceramic-coated rims, however.

Install new tires. Fresh rubber is another great way to improve your bike's performance. It'll make you feel all grippy and warm the next time you get on the dirt.

Tune your fork. If your suspension fork is more than a year old, chances are it could use fresh oil or an elastomer change. Just look for overhaul instructions in the fork manual that came with your bike. If you've lost it, check at your local bike shop for a replacement copy.

Watch videos. This isn't really working on your bike—it's working on your biking. You can buy an amazing array of cycling videos that range from classic road events to tips on mountain biking skills.

Go for a hike. It's not all about bikes, you know. Hang your steed, strap on your boots, and hit the trails. Hiking anywhere is cool, but it's extra cool to hike the trails you ride. It will give you an entirely new perspective and might even help you figure out how to ride a section that's been giving you fits.

A MATTER OF BALANCE

It's a simple relationship: If you lose your balance, you fall. But balance is more than just the thing that keeps you upright and intact. Balance is, as corporate-synergy specialists say, proactive. It has lots of benefits. You'll become a better mountain biker if you focus on the cool stuff that balance can do for you rather than learning just enough to avoid its detriments. This is the place to start if you want to improve your off-road riding.

The great riders possess a sense of balance so sharp that they almost meld with their bikes like centaurs. Instead of merely riding atop a machine, a balanced rider relates to his bike like it's another limb. He knows how to move his body to get through turns quicker, to keep the wheels on the ground for more stability (or lift them when necessary), to shoot across lines until he finds the best one, to pause momentarily during slow-speed sections so he can plan his attack.

In time, you'll learn most of this stuff, but it'll be easier if you already have an understanding of how your weight placement affects your bike's handling.

Here are four things you can start playing with right now.

Learn to do a trackstand. This is the act of balancing your bike at a standstill. It's simpler than it seems; in three or four practice sessions you should be able to pull off a 20- to 30-second trackstand. (The name, by the way, comes from a technique used on velodromes by track racers.) The secret is to really practice it. Most riders fool

Practice trackstands to develop great balance.

around with it only during downtime—before or after a ride. But if you dedicate 30 minutes at a time to this skill, you'll become a master.

Here how's to do it: Ride to a slight incline. Position your crankarms horizontally, then turn your front wheel slightly as you come to a stop. Apply just enough pedal pressure to keep yourself from rolling backward, but not so much that you roll forward. (If you do, straighten the front wheel slightly and let yourself roll back.) You can use the front brake if you want—people learn it both with and without the brake. It's not that tough. Once you have it, practice without the incline.

Ride with your eyes closed. But not on a trail. Go to a wide, long, unpopulated grassy field. Begin pedaling across it, then close your eyes for three pedal strokes. Work up to 10 or more if you can. The sensation is disconcerting, and riding blind is probably not a skill you'll ever use. But without your vision, you pay more attention to how the bike moves over terrain, and each sideways sway or forward dip becomes magnified. You get closer to being able to feel what the bike feels. You don't need to spend much time practicing this unless you enjoy the experience.

Ride on narrow spaces. Try a two-by-four laid flat, or a curb. Thin things are everywhere—ride them whenever you get the chance. Because you need to keep the bike rolling on such a narrow plane, you're forced to do all of your balancing with your body. You'll learn lots of little tricks of movement—the subtle counterbalances and opposing weights—that are impossible to explain but develop naturally. If you do these things wrong, your bike will fall off the curb, giving you instant feedback.

Dance with your bike. Move your body around to see how much you can make the bike match or oppose your movements. When you swing your body way far to the right, what does the bike do? How can you make it swing right with you? How can you make it tip to the left while you go right? Can you lift the rear wheel even if most of your weight is centered over it?

You can do this kind of monkeying around while you're waiting for your friends to show at the trailhead. The idea is to get your body and bike into awkward relationships and then figure out how to bring them under control again.

Finally, here's a benefit most riders don't realize: Besides greatly improving your slow-speed riding, this practice will pay off someday when you get all twisted up at high speed and realize that the situation actually feels familiar.

5

LOOSEN UP

One thing you hear a lot is that mountain bikers should "ride like water." The idea is a good one—flow naturally along the path of least resistance. Of course, water doesn't flow well uphill, so the image breaks down if you think about it too much. Even so, it's a good analogy, because it can help you visualize a mistake so many beginners make—riding like frozen water.

Tense mountain bikers ride like ice cubes. They bounce down a trail instead of flowing over it. Every shock from the ground is transmitted from the bike through their stiff limbs. Their steering is unpredictable. They fatigue quickly. They lack stability and control. They are uncomfortable.

If you can learn to keep your upper body calm and steady while the bike bobs and swerves beneath you, you'll start to flow, and your stiffness will melt away. This is a huge leap in your mountain biking ability, but it's a pretty easy thing to accomplish.

The key is riding in the "ready" position, also called the attack position, a stance that conserves much of your energy while letting the bike move under you. It keeps you poised to make any moves or shifts in balance that are necessary to handle the terrain. It's the neutral position you should return to after any juking, climbing, descending, or whatever—like returning to the baseline in tennis. Here's how.

Staying off the saddle is a key component of the "ready" position.

Flex your elbows and knees. Keep them flexed. That's how you absorb shock.

Keep your crankarms horizontal. A pedal that is down can catch on objects protruding from the trail. But horizontal feet give you an even platform to stand on, which helps you float around the bike.

Keep your butt above the saddle. A good mountain biker rarely sits during intense parts of a trail. He floats his butt over the seat, grazing it as a guide to know where the bike is more than using it as support. Conversely, if most of your weight is on the seat, every kick of the rear wheel kicks you. If you're floating, you can avoid the butt-bashing and also flick your body around to maintain balance.

Balance your contact points. You're searching for an exquisite balance—not so much off the saddle that most of your weight is on your feet (which tires your legs and makes your ride jerky), but not so loose in the elbows that you feel disconnected from the handlebar and planted on the saddle. Whenever you feel stuck on one part of the bike, redistribute your weight.

Monitor your hands, shoulders, and jaw. If any of these are clenched, you're probably riding stiffly instead of ready. Although it sounds counterintuitive, keeping a relatively loose grip on the handlebar will actually help you maintain control by letting the front end of the bike move slightly to follow the path of least resistance. Of course, don't go *too* loose: If one of your hands slips off the grip on a fast downhill, you're pretty much guaranteed some up-close-and-personal time with Ma Earth. Wearing gloves is one key to this technique, because sweaty palms are slippery palms.

6 》》》

PERFECT YOUR PEDALING

There are lots of big, obvious ways to become a better rider: Learn how to unweight the front wheel, learn how to lift the rear, or figure out that shifting thing. There are also a few small but important techniques. They aren't flashy, and chances are, none of your friends (except maybe the most skilled) will recognize that you have them. But these things will make a huge difference in how you ride.

One of the coolest techniques is learning to spin the pedals.

Mountain bikers tend to be mashers. They chop the pedals, pushing down with hard, heavy leg motions. This style looks impressive, but it robs power, because energy is being transmitted through less than half of the pedal stroke.

The idea is to deliver energy throughout as much of the pedal stroke as possible. You want to try—as impossible as it actually is—to pedal in smooth circles, with a seamless output of power. This raises your speed, increases traction (because the tire isn't jerking every time you stomp the pedals), uses less energy (which means you can ride longer), and even improves your balance and handling, because you're steadier on the bike. Not a bad list for a tiny skill. Here's how to make it happen.

Go around, not up and down. The next time you ride, pedal in a circle, focusing on one leg. Try it for 10 minutes while using a gear that gives you moderate pedaling resistance. Push down; before the pedal reaches the bottom of the stroke, pull back as if you're trying to scrape mud off the bottom of your shoe. Pull up. Just before the pedal reaches the top, start pushing it forward.

It's not really an even application of power all the way around—laboratory tests have shown that's impossible—but you powered the pedal much more than usual. The motion will feel strange at first, especially when you pull up. And your leg will tire quickly. When it does, switch to the other. When that one is shot, forget about circles and enjoy the rest of the ride. Do this two or three times a week, and in a month, you'll be a smoothie. (If you use toeclips and straps, you might have to tighten them to enable pulling back on the pedal.)

Spin faster, not harder. When you want to get a quick burst of speed—powering up a little hill, closing a gap, sprinting for the tape—tell yourself to pedal faster rather than harder. This will help you spin the pedals quicker rather than mashing them. It increases your speed while keeping you smooth. Of course, there are times when you do want a heavy, hard power stroke—like when you want to loft the front wheel, for instance.

Relax about cadence. Some people like to make a big deal out of finding the optimum cadence (the number of revolutions one foot makes in a minute, also called pedal rpm). At least 90 rpm on the flats, no lower than 75 on hills, blah, blah, blah.

That's fine for roadies, but on a vertical trail, you may never see the top side of 50 rpm. Most mountain bikers seem to have a natural flat-ground cadence of around 80 rpm, and perhaps you would ride better at a slightly higher rate. But it's more important to be smooth no matter what your cadence is. Any smooth rpm is better than the same number of jerky rpm. Too, a slightly lower (but still smooth and efficient) cadence will keep you from bouncing around excessively over bumpy terrain.

Adjust for fatigue. When your lungs are tired, slow your cadence. When your legs are tired, shift to a lower gear so you can speed it up. It works.

7

SPEED IS WHAT YOU NEED

Beginners live on the extremes. For instance, novices either ride way too slow or way too fast. In a strange way, it takes experience to find the middle ground.

Consider Bill, for instance. He was a slow beginner. Speed didn't scare him, but it made him uncomfortable. He told himself that once he learned to ride—after he mastered enough of the techniques—he would work on going faster. It sort of worked: Now he can ride pretty fast, pretty confidently.

Clark, a guy who started mountain biking just after Bill did, was the opposite type of new rider. Clark rode hard, heavy, and fast, trusting speed to carry him over things and get him out of messes that his skill couldn't. For instance, he couldn't bunny-hop the regular way, but he would launch off small rises at 20 mph. His idea was that he'd have the thrill first and learn the skill later. That sort of worked, too. Clark still isn't as sharp as Bill in technical sections, but he's a pretty good rider now. And he's earned a few more bumps and bruises along the way, which is either stupid or admirable, depending on your perspective.

Which approach is better? Neither, really. They're just different. Bill practiced technique until it became graceful instinct. Clark spent more time living on the glorious edge and became comfortable with the sensation of speed. Bill walked a lot of stuff early on. Clark bent rims and broke chainrings. Now, they're pretty much the same rider.

In hindsight, however, Bill says, "I wish I'd gone faster. I think if I'd ridden closer to the edge, challenged myself more, I'd be a better rider today. It's like the difference between eating right when you're a kid and when you're an adult. Childhood deficiencies stunt your growth for the rest of your life."

This chapter's advice is for everyone who seems to be following Bill's cautious path. These tips will help you ride faster sooner and get better quicker.

Make small movements. You might not feel comfortable at high speeds because you're still riding like you're going slow. The adjustments you make to your bike and body (turns, weight shifts, depressing the brake levers) should become smaller as you go faster. A tiny movement done quickly has a bigger impact than a big movement done slowly.

Look farther ahead. Five feet in front of your wheel? Ten feet? There's no right answer to how far ahead you should look. So much depends on speed, terrain, and your ability. Lots of new riders concentrate their vision in an area no more than 10 feet from the front of their wheels. When you start looking beyond—from 10 feet to the horizon—you'll begin going faster and feeling better about it. This works because your head stops concentrating on the immediate and begins planning for the next adventure. You've stopped reacting—which requires a slower pace—and started creating your own line.

Ride straighter. Slow means bobbing and turning, cool body English, and maneuvers. Fast means rolling over most things and evading only the very nasty. You can do this because you're like a speedboat instead of a dinghy. You're riding the crest of the trail's waves, smoothing it all out instead of dipping down into each feature.

Stay loose. It's natural to become tense. Consciously work against it. Keep your hands loose by twitching your fingers. Swallow and talk to yourself to unclench your jaw. Shake your elbows. Relaxing at speed is so much more important than it is when you go slow. If you hit something hard and stiff while you're cooking, it's you who'll be well done.

8 >>>

THEM'S THE BRAKES

Experienced off-roaders sometimes talk about a ride's rhythm— swooping and flowing along a trail, carried by a current that makes miles roll by effortlessly. It's a peak mountain bike experience that beginners taste only in small amounts. Why? Because clumsy braking interrupts the rhythm, which makes you slower and more prone to crashing.

Novices tend to use the brakes when they aren't needed. Even worse is not using them when they really *are* required. Controlled slowing is more than a matter of enjoyment—body parts hang in the balance. Here are some tips for avoiding both types of errors and for making the most of your brakes.

Memorize which brake is which. Sound too basic? Maybe. But even if you know that your right lever operates the rear brake (re- member the RR rule: right = rear) and the left controls the front, do you have to think about it?

Try this off-bike drill: Have a friend say "front" or "rear" while you squeeze the corresponding hand. If your instantaneous and instinctive reaction isn't correct 10 out of 10 times, repeat the drill for practice. It might sound silly, but it's safer than gaining this knowledge during a ride. (Although a single horrifying endo caused by a misapplied front brake will certainly imprint the correct actions in your brain.) Some riders swap the controls so the setup matches their gas-burning bikes.

Find a favorite finger arrangement. If you're haphazard about how you grip the brake levers, your attempts to stop will be unpredictable— weak one time, overpowering the next. Most mountain bikers use a two- finger grip: thumb, ring finger, and pinky on the handlebar, with the index and middle fingers on the lever. With the advent of hyperpowerful disc brakes, even this is often overkill: A single finger on the lever is ad-equate in all but the most on-the-edge situations.

Master the front brake. Yes, it has scary stopping power—up to 80 percent of your bike's total, enough to suddenly immobilize your bike and send you flying over the handlebar. For this reason, many novices avoid the front brake and try to slow themselves using only the rear brake, which is weaker. This can cause skidding and loss of control.

To get comfy with your left lever, try this drill in a grassy field. At a slow speed, mash the brake. If you do it hard enough, your rear wheel will rise off the ground. Don't panic. Just let go of the brake and you'll return to the ground. If you didn't tip forward, brake harder next time. Play around at different speeds to find the unbalancing point, then experiment with moving your body backward or forward.

Learn how hard to brake. Here's how your braking action should typically happen: Apply both brakes at the same time, putting slightly more pressure on the rear than the front at first, then increasing the front squeeze as necessary. But this changes with the surface. For in-stance, mushy terrain such as sand, gravel, or mud makes a hard-braking front wheel more likely to dig in. A great rule of thumb is to brake hard when the ground is hard, and soft when the ground is soft.

Braking force also changes with slope. Descending is covered in Chapter 24, but the main idea is that when your rear wheel begins to skid on a downhill, it's time to use more front brake.

Brake before a turn. Don't wait until midcorner to decide that you're going too fast. If you try to slow when your bike is leaning or when your front wheel is angled, you'll probably crash. The physics are bad—force and vectors and stuff like that. Brake to the right speed before you start to turn.

Figure out when not to brake. Let go of your levers a second sooner than usual when you come out of a turn. You'll feel a surge of speed. Try to scrub off speed by riding up a bank instead of squeezing a lever. You'll feel a smooth swoop instead of a staccato slowing. That's the ride rhythm mentioned earlier, and it can happen only when you have enough confidence in your braking ability to know when not to use it.

Use a two-finger grip for consistent braking.

Note to boneheads: This concept is not the same as hurtling down a technical descent at 50 mph on your third-ever mountain bike ride. Be judicious.

9

TURN WITHOUT TURNING

The term "turn" is almost a misnomer for the part of a trail that changes direction, because to get your bike through one you don't really turn anything. Except at slow speeds—walking pace or less—the position of your handlebar doesn't change much as you ride through a corner. You do what you need to do mostly by leaning your bike and body. Here's how to carve crisp turns.

Before You Turn

Reduce the sharpness of a turn and the amount you must lean (both moves improve traction, especially on loose surfaces) by riding as direct a line as possible. You're trying to "straighten" the curve by slicing off the top. Approach wide, cut to the inside at the apex, and exit wide—as much as you can. On a dirt road, you can do much more straightening than you can on singletrack.

Adjust your line for terrain. If the wide/inside/wide line passes through a minefield of sharp rocks, seek a smoother inside (or farther outside) line. Pick your line before entering the turn, and then stick with it. Trying to switch in midturn is almost always slower and is usually dangerous because it unbalances your bike.

Adjust your speed before the turn. If you try to brake while you're leaning, you're likely to skid. Or the bike could slip right out from under you. So if your approach speed exceeds your comfort zone, brake before turning starts. It's safer and more effective.

Level the crankarms. Stop pedaling and position your crankarms horizontally (parallel to the ground). This keeps them from catching on the outside bank, a rock, or other obstacles. On smooth surfaces, you can keep the outside pedal down to improve traction.

While You Turn

Press down on the handlebar with your inside hand and lean the bike in that direction. For tight corners taken at slow speed, you might need to subtly turn the handlebar toward the inside—but not very much. It's almost always less than an inexperienced rider anticipates.

Some riders like to begin their lean by "countersteering." This means that you quickly cut the bike in the opposite direction of the turn (for instance, for a right turn, twitch the handlebar to the left). Your body instinctively compensates for the swerve by causing the bike to pitch back over in the proper direction and dive into the turn at a sharper angle than you would otherwise achieve. Because it's done by instinct, it's easier than it sounds.

Increase traction. You need to drive your wheels into the ground with body weight and leg force to counteract the sideways momentum that wants to pull your bike out from under you. The best way is to put the outside pedal down and stand on it hard. If you need to keep the pedals horizontal because of uneven terrain, however, you'll have to put enough opposing force on the inside pedal to keep them both parallel to the ground. If the surface is smooth enough to let you put lots of weight on an outside pedal that's down, you can get much better traction.

Fine-tune your line. Once you enter the turn, you don't want to switch lines completely. But it's common to have to slightly adjust your line because your speed is slightly too fast or slow to carry you out of the turn where you plan, or because of unforeseen obstacles or changes in the trail surface. Don't use your handlebar. This can turn the tire and force it against your momentum—you'll crash. Instead, swing your elbow or knee toward the inside corner. It's like when a bird turns by twitching a feather.

Position the crankarms horizontally in turns to avoid obstacles.

After You Turn

After passing the apex, begin pedaling. Do it right, and you'll feel like the turn flings you out on the trail. If you do it too soon, your inside pedal will scrape the ground. Do it too late, and you won't get flung. And flung is fun.

Straighten up. Gently press your outside hand down on the handlebar to come out of the lean. This weight shift is instinctive.

Set up for the next turn. As you're coming out of one corner, you should be positioning your bike to go wide/inside/wide for the next turn. As always, you need to be looking and thinking well ahead.

GET OVER IT!

Almost anyone can get over little logs, rocks, and bumps—say 6 to 8 inches tall—as soon as they start riding. But getting over a thing isn't the same as rolling over a thing. Instead of wobbling before and after obstacles, stuttering halfway over, and disrupting the rhythm and momentum of your ride (like most beginners), you should skim over stuff with small, smooth movements.

The key to divine rolling is that you don't just roll. Even obstacles as tiny as 2 inches high can be ridden smoothly if you adopt a choreography of weight shifts and momentum control.

The following steps are all you need to become a skimmer instead of a pounder. In just a few attempts, you'll be a smoothie on anything less than 8 inches high. To get over bigger stuff, you need to start doing wheelies. And as you get better, you'll begin popping wheelies over the small stuff, too. But the light and smooth rollover is ideal for novices.

Approach with momentum. Most inexperienced bikers go so slowly that their bikes stuff up when they hit an object, or stall halfway over. Use this guideline: Go fast enough so that even if you don't pedal for the final 2 feet of approach, you'll still clear the obstacle.

Keep your hands off the brakes. This isn't how you're supposed to ride, but it is how you're supposed to learn. When you're practicing rolling over stuff, your brain sometimes panics and tells your hands to jam on the brakes. But when you do that, you flip over the handlebar. After you're confident enough riding over things to ignore your screaming brain, ride with one or two fingers on the brake levers in all situations.

Be the dough, not the cookie. You want to be in a position that lets you absorb the bike as it rises up into your body. Cookies crumble. Dough absorbs. And then it pops back into place. So keep your elbows and knees flexed, your crankarms horizontal, and your butt floating just above the saddle. This is the ready position described in Chapter 5.

Unweight the front wheel, but keep it steady. Move your body slightly to the rear to lighten the front of the bike. A heavy front wheel will stick when it hits the object instead of rolling up and over. But you don't want the front so light that the wheel is unsteady and turns to one side when it hits the obstacle. Keep your grip firm enough to make sure that the wheel climbs instead of turns.

Absorb the impact. When your front wheel hits, stay relaxed and let the bike rise toward your

A light front wheel will help the bike roll over an object.

chest. Your elbows, which were partially extended, will bend more deeply. Your knees will do the same thing.

Return to the ready position. When the front wheel comes off the obstacle and hits the ground, return your arms to their original position, which helps bring over the rear. Shift your weight forward again, returning to the neutral position. This unweights your rear wheel so it, too, rolls over lightly instead of smashing into the obstacle.

ROUGH STUFF

What makes mountain biking mountain biking? It isn't mountains; there are some great rides in the Hoosier flatland kingdom of Indiana. And it isn't dirt, which can be packed as hard as a macadam highway.

The answer lies around the word "smoothness." Mountain biking is the lack of it. A true off-road experience is about bumps and jumps and lumps and humps. You're up and down and in and out. Here's how to thrive on some of the most common surfaces: compressions, rollers, washboards, and steps.

Compressions

Ditches, dips, gullies, gulches, and sharp-walled holes with no fancy name are called compressions because that's what they do to you—slam the bike up into your body. If you don't know how to absorb this impact, you eat your handlebar, then wipe your face in the dirt. It's unsightly.

To ride slowly through a compression, shift your weight slightly rearward as you enter the hole. Level the crankarms and straighten your own arms (without locking your elbows), pushing the front wheel down into the dip. When you hit bottom, flex your arms and legs to pull the bike back up and absorb the impact. You've pushed the bike away and then pulled it back, instead of letting the hole take control of these actions. You're in charge.

Hit the pedals with one hard power stroke to lift the front wheel and set it atop the other side of the hole. As soon as it clears the edge, press down on the front to maintain traction and control. Shift your weight forward, let the rear wheel come up lightly behind you, and you're out.

You can also speed through compressions. This is cool, but it's also dangerous. Before your front wheel drops into the hole, lift it by pulling up with your arms as you give a power stroke and shift your weight back. Your goal is to never let your front wheel dip into the hole. Your rear wheel will drop down, but by then you should have landed your front wheel beyond the dip. Shift your weight forward so you don't smash the rear wheel against the side of the hole. This is a fast but risky move. Make sure you're ready for it.

Rollers

A roller is a short, severe rise that, unlike a true climb, isn't long enough to make you regret ever starting it. You can't pedal over a roller because it's too steep. The key to cleaning these sharp rises is to approach with enough speed to coast to the crest. That's probably way more speed than seems smart. There's no guideline for choosing the proper speed. If you stall out, you didn't have enough.

As you coast up, keep your crankarms horizontal to prevent catching a pedal on the peak. Once you're at the crest, push the handlebar down by extending your elbows. This forces your bike to start down the other side, making sure that you don't end up teetering on the top in limbo.

Experienced riders may kick their bikes down the other side by giving a swift half-pedal stroke, then leveling the crankset again. This is cool because it adds momentum, but it's usually too much for new riders to think about. Just concentrate on pushing your bike down the other side until you understand the rhythm involved.

Washboards

The corduroy of nature never goes out of fashion. Long stretches of rippled surface will rattle your organs and batter your hands after just a few seconds. But if you remember not to tighten up from all the shaking, there's not much danger.

Keep a secure (not clenched) grip on the handlebar. Rise slightly out of the saddle, bend your knees and elbows, and let the bike jitter beneath you. If you have the right technique, your head will remain on about the same plane while your bike bucks. If your vision blurs, you're riding too tight.

Fast turns on washboard are for expert riders. Slow down and live to ride another day. The problem is that your tires have trouble getting traction to turn as they're bouncing across the rippled surface. You can make your tires hook up (regain traction), but it takes guts and knowledge of how your balance affects the bike's motion.

Don't tense up when riding on washboard terrain.

Steps

Descending steps—whether they're made by forces of nature or concrete mixers—is much more impressive-looking than it is difficult. In fact, this is probably the first hard-looking skill any novice can master. Learning to shift your weight to hop a 6-inch log is tougher than learning to ride a staircase. But steps look harder, so not many new riders try them. Boost your reputation by practicing this technique on a set of 8 to 10 steps. Any fewer and the ride ends before you can figure out what's happening.

As you approach the first drop, shift your weight rearward. Let the front wheel roll over. Don't push it down with your arms like you do for compressions. Then, give your bike the freedom it needs to bounce its way down. Basically, you're just along for the ride, absorbing the shock by flexing your knees and elbows so your body doesn't interfere with the bike's downward patter. The hits won't be big but they'll come rapidly, so you need to work your arms and legs faster than you're used to.

If you gain too much speed, lightly apply the front brake—but keep in mind that going too slow is more likely to crash you than going too fast. If you stall the bike, you won't be able to get a foot down on the angled and uneven surface.

12 >>>

SLIPPERY SURFACES

Although you should always try to ride smoothly, you shouldn't always ride on smooth things. Rock fields throw you into new lines every 2 seconds, roots chatter your body and are lethal when wet, and patches of ooze sluice your wheels sideways—funky stuff is cool.

Learning to traverse weird terrain makes you a better bike handler, a braver person, and one of those riders who doesn't stop when others do. Here's some advice to help get you over rocks, roots, and mud—three tough challenges that can send your wheel slip-sliding away.

Rocks

As you approach a patch of hard, pointy things, get off the saddle until your butt just grazes it, and be sure that your knees and elbows are flexed—you need room for your bike to jackhammer beneath you. Begin planning a line that lets you enter and exit in as straight a line as possible, because turns and curves often aren't executable in rocks (at least not on purpose). If you have a choice, choose a line with larger, embedded rocks instead of small, loose stones, which will roll and scatter beneath your wheels.

As you enter, maintain enough momentum to smooth out some of the bumps. Think about trying to skim the tops of the bumps. If you go too slow, your bike will really punch you. Of course, if you go too fast, your line will outrun your skill and you'll do a number on your head. Between the extremes is a passage smoother than you can imagine. There's no prescription for the ideal speed. Keep giving yourself more as long as the ride keeps getting smoother.

When you're on the rocks, steer with your hips instead of the handlebar. Don't swing your entire body from side to side. You want to stay centered over your bike for more stability. And keep your front wheel straight. Don't give it a chance to wedge sideways between rocks. Be ready for it to slip down their angled sides.

Pedal in a gear that emphasizes muscle over spin. This keeps you off the saddle and helps nail the bike to the ground. Keep driving the rear wheel. Propulsion will solve some problems that your handling ability can't. The pedals will probably bang off rocks. Let it happen, let the bike juke sideways, and keep going.

When you go offline—and you will—go with the new flow. You might be able to fight your way back to your original line, but sometimes the rocks know more than you do. The terrain might be funneling you into a more natural route. But if you're on an obviously dangerous or impossible line, stop.

Roots

If tree roots grew perpendicular across trails, there would be no fun. We would just ride right over them. So all roots slant across trails, which means that our wheels skate along the slick wood, slide out from under us, and dump us. Fast . . . and hard. At any speed above walking pace, slipping on a root is one of those experiences that's over before you know it happened, and then you know it happened long after it's over.

Try to square off your approach to roots whenever you can (like a roadie going over railroad tracks). Even if they're wet, you can get over them if you cross at something close to a right angle. If you can't line it up, pick up the front wheel and set it back down on the other side of the root. This isn't a full wheelie; you don't want to spend that much time in the air. Just pull the handlebar more back than up.

Sometimes you can square up your rear wheel after the front is over. If not, hop the rear, too—again, just enough to clear the root. Lift with your feet, twist your wrists forward, and slightly move your weight to the front. Bunny-hops are cool, but make sure you won't land on more roots, because you're not going to stay up if that happens.

If you're facing an entire section of roots, get off and walk. But if you're feeling brave, enter with enough momentum to roll through without pedaling. Torque is your enemy. Brakes are your enemy, too. A motionless or dragged wheel is a skating fool.

Mud

First, the warning: Most mud is like the mucous membrane of the Earth, all moist and tender and rippable. Don't do anything to the Earth that you wouldn't do to your own orifices. Stay off slopes that end in ponds or streams, trails where water collects or runs in your tracks, trails where you leave tracks anywhere except in low spots, or

Treacherous surfaces that are ridden improperly will help you learn new tricks.

anywhere you know there's a chance that the ruts you make will freeze or become permanent gouges.

Some mud is eternal. You can ride that mud. If you can't tell the difference, ask someone who can. Stay off it in the meantime.

To roll through muck, slide rearward just before you enter it. If you're a light rider, shift to a lower gear and spin through the goo like a paddlewheeler. Keep your pedal strokes smooth so you have traction throughout the revolution, and try to keep your body weight floating over the bike instead of loading the wheels.

Large riders should forget the finesse; it won't work. Just sink to the bottom and grind across. Use a gear you can muscle, and drive your weight down into the bike for better traction. It's an ugly sight, but it's effective.

No matter what your style, keep the front wheel lighter than the rear. If you force it into the muck, the wheel may deflect sideways or stick and flip you. Either scenario creates an especially spectacular splash.

13

PEDAL SMARTS

Once upon a time, only expert mountain bikers in dry climates wore shoes with special cleats that clicked into the pedals, securing their feet like ski bindings. Beginners and intermediate riders were afraid they wouldn't be able to remove their feet quickly enough to avoid crashes, and riders in wet regions couldn't find pedals that operated well when filled with muck. But the fact is, clipless pedals are actually far safer than toe clips and straps, because they create a much more secure connection to the bike. With your feet clipped in, you'll have greater control and be able to maneuver your bike in ways that are impossible (or next to impossible) with clips and straps.

Today, there are clipless pedals that provide reliable security and release even in rotten weather and sloppy conditions. These pedal systems aren't a necessity—you can still get good riding performance with toeclips and straps—but clipless pedals are no longer for elitists. Even first-timers buy bikes equipped with clipless pedals. Here are some steps for making them user-friendly.

Trim the sole. If your shoe has big treads, it might be interfering with your ability to enter or exit your pedals. Try this: Click into one pedal, then take your foot out of the shoe. Flip the pedal over and examine everywhere the shoe and pedal touch. Treads that appear squashed or bent are probably creating resistance when you push your foot down to snap in or pivot it to click out. Remove the shoe and trim the problem areas with a utility knife.

Clean and lube it. Like any moving part of your bike, the retention device in the pedal must be kept spiffy. But use a light, dry lube or you'll attract more grit than you removed. It won't hurt to chisel last summer's mud away from the cleat, either.

Check for wear. If you're becoming plagued by inconsistent entry and exit, look at your cleats. If they're jagged or asymmetrical, it's time to replace them. Their life spans can be less than a season. It's counterintuitive, but worn cleats release more stubbornly, not more easily.

Become a stiffy. "Dual purpose" shoes intended to accommodate hiking as well as biking usually don't work as well, because they're more flexible, which means they give when you try to click in or out. This is something else that adds to inconsistency. Stick to shoes made specifically for mountain biking, which have stiffer soles but are still fine for short walks.

Practice odd click-outs. Ideally, you would need to click out only when your pedal is at the bottom of the stroke—the most common point for exiting. But in the real world, you'll need to dab when your pedals are in many different locations. So practice clicking out from the top of a pedal stroke, halfway down, and halfway up, and do it with each foot. You'll get the best results when you pivot your foot in the same plane as the pedal, rather than pulling back or up as you pivot.

Get used to clicking in. Fumbling a pedal entry won't cause as many wrecks as slow exits, but it's frustrating, embarrassing, absolutely disastrous if you've stopped in midclimb, and will eventually result in the pedal swinging around and piledriving into your shin. So practice. Most misfires occur because the cleat is not aligned with the retention device in the pedal. On the top of your shoe, make a small mark that aligns with the pedal axle when you're clicked in, and use that as a guide.

Get the right pedals. Different pedal models have different levels of "float," which is the lateral free play you get before your cleat releases. People with sensitive knees should look for as much float as possible, because float allows your knee to find its natural (and hopefully pain-free) angle. But more float also makes it more difficult to release from the pedal in emergency situations, because you have to move your foot through the float range before your cleat disengages. For that reason, low-float pedals are easier for beginning riders to learn on.

14 ⟫⟩⟩⟩

EAT YOUR ENERGY

Nutrition can get pretty complicated, especially when experts start blabbing about stuff like electrolytes, antioxidants, and creatine. Maybe the pros need to monitor their fuel intakes like scientists mixing a batch of shuttle fuel, but most riders just want to know how to keep going strong without vomiting or fainting. Thankfully, that's a pretty simple order.

What most novices perceive as a lack of fitness is really a lack of energy. When your tank hits "E," you suffer from leg cramps, fading concentration, bad mojo, and other ills. If you keep yourself fed and watered, you can pedal farther than you ever imagined. Here are the basics for doing that.

Take in mostly carbo. Carbohydrate is the best source of cycling fuel, because it's easily transformed into glucose and glycogen—the stuff your muscles burn. Fat is also used for energy, but it's less efficient. Protein isn't a good burn, either. So your diet should be mostly carbo—60 to 70 percent of total calories. Fat should be 20 to 30 percent, and protein the remaining 10 to 15 percent. You can count if you want to, but an easier method is to just make sure you don't eat a lot of stuff that tastes too good.

You won't need to chow during a ride unless you're going for more than a couple of hours. You have enough sugar stored in your blood and muscles to fuel shorter efforts.

Eat before you're hungry. Begin nibbling a half hour into your epic ride so that putty bar has time to get through your stomach, get converted into energy, and be used by your muscles. If you wait to eat until you actually feel hungry, you'll never catch up with your hard-working body's energy requirements.

Consume just enough. If you stuff yourself, blood will be diverted from your muscles to your bloated digestive system. Cramping, fol-

You'll need to eat on a ride if you're out for more than 2 hours.

lowed by vomiting, is the likely result. Most people need only about 20 grams of carbo for every 20 minutes of riding. That's two bananas per hour, a packet of energy gel, or most of an energy bar. Nibble, don't gorge.

Go for what you like. Almost all of the commercial energy snacks have just the right mix of carbohydrate, fat, and protein. Some of them have lots of other nutrients, too. Others market their naturalness. Whatever you buy, just make sure it's something you like to eat, or you'll never take in enough energy.

Drink before you're thirsty. It's that never-catch-up phenomenon again. Sip from your bottle or hydration backpack at least every 15 minutes, and at the top of most hills. Watch the color of your urine. If it's nearly clear, you're good. If your output is yellow, drink more. If you're standing around dry while everyone else is off wetting the bushes, drink lots more. If your eyes are sunk so far into your head it's like looking through tunnels, go to the hospital and get an IV. Use a sports drink instead of plain water to get extra carbo calories plus those arcane substances called electrolytes that help prevent muscle cramps by replenishing the chemicals lost in sweat.

Use your glycogen window. Immediately after a ride, your body has superhuman abilities to transform food into stored energy. Replenish your wasted muscles right away. After an hour or so, the window begins to close. You need about a half gram of carbo for every pound you weigh. For most of us, that's about one banana and half a bagel. You can also get what you need from a sports drink, special carbo-replenishment formula, or chocolate chip cookies. Actually, you can get a lot more than you need from those. But that's part of the fun, right?

15 ⟫⟫⟫

BREATHE RIGHT

Muscles alone will not get you up the trail. Breathing supplies the oxygen that makes those well-trained quads work. But many riders can't control the simple act of respiration. They don't know how to breathe efficiently, so they waste energy and gasp uncomfortably on climbs.

At bike camps in Colorado where top masters athlete **Skip Hamilton** of Aspen is an instructor, he sees riders fly in from sea level, and the next day they're laboring up trails at 10,000 feet. Here's how Hamilton helps them deal with the difficulty—a technique that works for all riders, no matter what the altitude.

"There's no better time to get riders to pay attention to their breathing than when they're gasping like fish out of water. I ride alongside and explain how to get the most out of every breath. My approach, called switch-side breathing, produces almost miraculous increases in climbing speed and comfort—and it's easy to learn. I picked it up from Ian Jackson, author of *BreathPlay,* when we used to go snowshoe running around Aspen. Then I started using it on the bike.

"No one is quite sure why switch-side breathing works. When I was a mountain runner, I noticed that a runner's injuries would often be on the same side. For example, his right knee, ankle, and hamstring all hurt. And the injuries often coincided with his dominant breathing side. But when we taught him switch-side breathing, his injuries went away. Apparently, if you always breathe on one side, you may subconsciously exert more force on that side. Switch-side breathing balances out the effort of the legs and makes climbing easier. Give it a try."

Breathe from your belly. Start by practicing correct athletic breathing off the bike. Lie on your back on the floor with a book on your stomach. Breathe in slowly and fully, expanding your diaphragm, not your chest. The book should move toward the ceiling. Then exhale steadily so it moves down toward the floor.

Most people think they should expand their chests, as a drill sergeant does. But if you look at side-view photos of professional roadies like Lance Armstrong or Italy's Ivan Basso, their bellies almost look fat. Their diaphragms are expanded like bullfrogs in full voice. It may look funny, but it leaves more room for air to get into the lungs.

Be a switch-hitter. Try the technique on the bike. Most riders exhale on the same side of the pedal stroke every time. If you're right-handed, you probably breathe out when the right pedal starts the downstroke. You can check by climbing a flight of stairs and paying attention to your pattern. Once you get a rhythm going, I'll bet you exhale each time the same foot hits a step.

The easiest way to break out of this pattern of same-side breathing is simply to take an extra-long out-breath every 5 to 10 pedal strokes. That will automatically switch your out-breath to the other downstroke. Try it several times on long climbs and it will start to become second nature. Practice off the bike whenever you walk up a long flight of stairs. While you're climbing stairs, your foot strike is slower and more pronounced than in cycling, This makes it easier to coordinate with your breathing.

Exhale with vigor. Finally, emphasize the out-breath. If you force air out of your lungs, you won't even need to think about breathing in. You'll get full, deep breaths and avoid shallow, inefficient panting. Even better, it will happen automatically. Some good riders even make a guttural sound as they breathe out, like weight lifters. They might sound like a pig in a pen when they climb, but it works.

16

END YOUR BEGINNING

At some point, you get sick of being a beginner. How do you get to the next level?

There's no test, no exam, no official Bureau of Mountain Biking representative who reviews your ride and approves or rejects your application. You stop being a new rider when you decide that you are now an intermediate one.

The catalyst for the transition might be anything. You finally make it up the local killer hill. You whomp your friend a good one. Someone even goofier than you shows up for the group ride. Ka-boom! Something in your head shakes loose and you no longer consider yourself a novice. Congrats.

But guess what? Although you are—as officially as it gets in this sport—an intermediate, you might still spend most of your time riding like a beginner. A lot of people do. In fact, most of the skills are the same. Intermediates just refine the basic moves to go a little faster, a little smoother, a little farther. It's not until the next step—expert—that you begin to learn totally new techniques.

Even so, the difference between a beginner ride and an intermediate ride is not merely a matter of gradual and amorphous refinement. An intermediate ride has two elements you never experience in your beginner rides: anticipation and linking. These two things aren't exactly tips; they're concepts, ideas. Even so, you can incorporate them into your riding style.

Anticipation

Don't think of anticipation simply as seeing what's ahead before it gets to you. That's a basic vision technique—one of the first things you learn is to look beyond your front wheel so you don't get surprised and so you have time to pick out a good line. Anticipation is more. It's about identifying a section's peak move—the spot that will require the most finesse or muscle, or both. Or the part of a racecourse where the greatest gain can be made. Or the patch of local trail where the most fun can be found.

Whatever the qualifier, the section maxes the scale. Anticipation is a self-choreographed approach to that peak move. Instead of riding the best line move by move, you ride for the best peak line.

Novices think: "Log . . . log . . . riser . . . avoidable rock . . . juke into the shallow end of the stream . . . uphill lunge. . . ."

Intermediates think: "Log. . . . log . . . riser and come down hammering so I can bop over the rock to set up to go straight through the deeper part of the stream so my wheel bites the big log with better traction instead of sinking into the loose stuff right before the peak uphill lunge. . . ."

That's anticipation.

Linking

This is when riders hook their moves together—like lifting the front wheel and shifting it to one side at the same time for a wheelie turn, instead of wheelie first, turn next.

There are all kinds of linked moves—

Are you ready for the next level?

too many to list. What's important is that you become aware that you should link. Stop concentrating so hard on one technique at a time. Sometimes, you can even stop concentrating at all. Let yourself improvise and see what happens.

In a way, linking is connected to anticipation. Pick that peak move, then let your bike flow mindlessly up to it. At the peak move, draw on everything you know—use your skill. Before that point, let your skill use you. You're the transmitter between the technique and the bike. The mindless flow is where you'll begin linking. Eventually, you'll link at the peak moves, pulling combinations to get through situations that once seemed improbable. Or even impossible.

ASK UNCLE KNOBBY

"What does it mean when someone says that a bike has a replaceable derailleur hanger?"

It means good news for the bike's owner. The derailleur hanger is the part of the frame where the rear derailleur bolts on. This is a vulnerable spot. If the derailleur catches on some trail debris and pretzels itself, the twisting force can sometimes bend the hanger at the same time. On steel bikes, this is usually not a lethal problem, because the hanger can simply be bent back to its original position. But you can't reshape aluminum or carbon fiber that way, so your frame is trash. To prevent this, most bike makers attach special hangers that will break off before the frame bends. Then you can simply buy a new hanger instead of a new frame.

"Is it uncool to use the granny gear?"

Not at all. The granny gear is the pairing of your smallest chainring with the largest cassette cog. This results in the easiest pedaling gear, so some dopes think it's wimpy to use it. There's no shame in visiting granny, however (even pro racers do it sometimes), because it's helpful for conserving energy or riding up really steep sections. You'll do better on such climbs if you shift into the granny gear and spin rather than try to muscle up the slope in a harder gear.

"What is an apex and why is it important?"

The apex is the part of a turn that's most pronounced—its peak. It's important because how you ride through the apex affects the whole turn.

Early-apex turns are the most common kind. It's a mistake to turn this way, but it's easy to understand why it happens. Most riders start to turn as soon as they see the turn. This leads to overturning, where you've turned so much so early that you're forced to move inside, brake, and slow too much.

A mid-apex turn is the fastest kind of turn. It's where the apex of your travel coincides with the physical apex of the turn. You ride to the widest point and change your direction of travel there. It's a gentle turn that sweeps you around a curve.

Late-apex turns are excellent when you want to pass somebody in a corner or scare the bejeebers out of one of your riding buddies. Even though you have to brake late in this turn in order to cut speed and dive through, you usually come out ahead of the next guy. These turns are great on banked surfaces, which help you keep more speed.

"What's the trick to getting my minipump to work?"

If you have tubes with a Presta valve (the long, skinny type with the little cap that must be unscrewed before inflating), you're probably not breaking the air lock before you try to pump. Often, if you don't depress the cap after you unscrew it, air pressure holds the valve shut so tightly that you can't get the new air in. Simply give the cap a quick tap to let out a shot of air.

Whether you have Presta or Schrader valves (the same kind as on car tires), you might not be seating the chuck properly. (The chuck is the valve fitting on the business end of the pump.) Some chucks have a tighten/loosen lever. Make sure this lever is in the loose position before you fit the chuck on the valve stem, then flip it to the tight position before you begin pumping. If there's no lever, just make sure that you press the chuck on far enough for a good seal.

Caution: Pressing the chuck too far onto a Presta valve will depress the cap and release high-pressure air back into the pump, possibly breaking it.

Sometimes, the action of pumping loosens the chuck, and air starts to escape. To prevent this, position your wheel so the valve is at a spot that lets you pump with minimal yanking and twisting. Usually, this is at the top.

"I just replaced a tube and now the new one won't hold air. What happened?"

Always feel around the inside of the tire to make sure whatever caused the original flat isn't still sticking through the tread. If that's not the reason for flat number two, then you probably pinched the new tube against the rim with your tire levers. This puts a nice little slit in the tube. To prevent it next time, you can inflate the tube slightly more, giving it a rounder profile that's less likely to catch under the lever; be more careful, checking for clearance before you pry with the lever; or stop using tire levers. Most mountain bike tires can be mounted entirely by hand—especially if they've been ridden for a while. Work section by section, pushing the tire up and over the rim with your thumbs.

"What can I do to improve my steering?"

Place a rock on smooth ground, and make figure-eight turns around it in different patterns. Pass the front wheel on the outside of the rock, and the back wheel on the inside. Then, pass both wheels on the outside, with the rear wheel coming as close to the rock as possible. Finally, pass the front wheel around the outside of the rock, rolling over it with the rear wheel. Practice both left and right turns, because most people naturally favor one side and are more awkward with the other. To keep rolling through the turn, move the bike smoothly and steadily. That's traction. The drill is a little dull, but it really works.

"What's the difference between hydraulic and mechanical disc brakes? And which are best for me?"

Hydraulic disc brakes use hydraulic brake fluid to contract their calipers, just like the disc brakes on your car or motorcycle. Mechanical disc brakes, on the other hand, utilize a wire cable, just like the standard rim brakes on many bicycles. Which is better? Well, if you value outright performance over mechanical simplicity, go with hydraulic: They tend to be smoother, easier to modulate, and have more

power. However, they do demand a higher degree of mechanical apti-
tude. Hydraulic brakes need to be bled every so often to remove air
from the lines, and they can leak through seals in the lever or caliper.
They're also pricey, as much as $200 per wheel. Meanwhile, cable-
activated discs offer much of the performance of hydraulics without
the mechanical complexity. Adjustments are no more complicated than
they are on rim brakes (meaning that you—yes, you!—can easily dial
them in) and they cost about half as much as hydraulics.

**"My mountain biking buddies keep talking about shocks with
'pedaling platforms' and 'motion control.' What the heck do they mean?"**

What they mean, my friend, is that suspension is finally living up to
its promise of downhill performance with minimal effect on uphill pedaling. Earlier generations of suspension were negatively affected by
hard pedaling efforts, meaning that shocks would move when riders
least wanted them to, siphoning off precious human energy. But recent
advances in suspension technology have led to shocks that are mini-
mally affected by pedaling forces, while retaining all their bump-eating
prowess. The result is a new generation of full-suspension bikes that
climb with near-hardtail efficiency and descend like demons. If you
haven't ridden a modern full-suspension bike, you haven't experienced
everything mountain bike technology has to offer.

**"I'm not a very aggressive rider. Do I really need full
suspension?"**

Well, no one *needs* full suspension. Of course, no one really needs
a mountain bike in the first place. Look, I'm just going to cut straight
to the chase: If you ride off-road (sounds obvious, but not everyone who
rides a mountain bike rides it off-road) and can afford a decent full-
suspension bike, buy one. Even casual riders can benefit from the
added control, comfort, and speed. Heck, casual riders benefit the
most from these things. How do you know if it's a decent bike? Well,
there really aren't that many bad ones out there anymore. It really boils
down to price: Good full-suspension bikes start at about $1,100, while
good hardtails can be had for about $300 less. If you simply can't dig
that deep, look at the used market. Even a gently used mountain bike
loses about 40 percent of its value in a single year.

"What are these little levers on my hubs all about?"

An improperly closed quick-release lever—the thing that runs through the hub and clamps the wheel to the bike—is one of the most dangerous things in cycling. (Second only to the drunk who lost his driver's license and now pilots his ancient 10-speed around town.)

Although some high-end, lightweight quick-releases are fastened by spinning, you should never try to secure a typical lever this way. Instead, close the lever by pivoting it with the palm of your hand. Many brands even have the words "open" and "closed" imprinted on opposite sides. Whichever word faces out indicates the lever's position.

If you don't feel resistance when the lever is half-closed (perpendicular to the wheel), open it again. Hold the lever in one hand, reach around the wheel to the other end of the quick-release, and screw in the nut on that end (clockwise). Try closing the lever again. When you feel resistance halfway, close the lever entirely. It should be pointing up and a bit to the rear so it won't snag something on a tight trail.

"Is 'singletrack' just another name for a trail?"

Nope. Singletrack is a type of trail wide enough for only one bike—like a single-file hiking trail or footpath. Anything wider is either a doubletrack, dirt road, or fire road. Technically, doubletrack refers to a trail made of parallel singletracks—like the wheel ruts created by pickups or sport-utility vehicles—but increasingly, it's used to refer to any wide trail. A dirt road is just what it sounds like. A fire road is a dirt road (great for fast downhill jamming) in the forest built for emergency vehicles. Um, don't hit one.

"What is chain slap?"

It's what happens when a too-slack chain bangs against the chainstay (the frame tube that runs from the rear dropout to the bottom bracket). Chain slap can chip or scratch paint and even cause the chain to derail. It most often occurs when the bike is bouncing on descents.

To prevent it, shift onto the middle or big chainring and one of the larger cogs. This wraps the chain around more teeth, which makes it tighter and unable to slap against the frame.

"My suspension fork has an adjustment for damping. So?"

So use it. You need to help your fork work its best for your weight and riding style as well as the terrain. Damping (and please don't call it "dampening") determines how quickly your fork compresses or rebounds when you hit a bump. Damping can be increased to slow the speed of your fork's action (which makes performance better on big bumps), or damping can be decreased to boost the action (which makes the fork more responsive to lots of smaller bumps). A good way to find the right adjustment is to ride the same section of trail several times, making damping changes before each pass.

FREERIDING: MOUNTAIN BIKING'S NEW FACE

It's impossible to say exactly when it began, but sometime in the early to mid-'90s, strange things started happening in the lush, coastal forests around Vancouver, British Columbia. Weary of the relatively tame cross-country trails they'd been riding for years, an audacious group of riders began looking for new ways to push the limits of the terrain and their skills. They took to the forests with saws and hammers and, melding natural and man-made materials, constructed tall, narrow ladder bridges, wild teeter-totters, and huge drops. The industry responded in kind, building bikes with copious suspension travel and burly frames designed to withstand the punishment of 10-foot drops onto rock and root.

Somewhere along the way, the term "freeriding" was coined to describe this new, no-boundaries style. The timing was perfect: Cross-country mountain biking was stagnating following the frenzy of its 1996 Olympic debut, and riders were hungry for something new.

Freeriding spread like a virus, sweeping south and east across the United States. Soon, riders from California to Connecticut were incorporating stunts into their trails and tackling terrain that only a few years before would have been considered impossible.

There's no concrete definition for freeriding; it can be pretty much anything you want it to be. But it is generally accepted that freeriding includes foreboding terrain that may or may not have been spiced up with man-made stunts or "features." These can include the aforementioned ladder bridges, teeter-totters, and drops, but also might simply be downed trees or natural rock faces. In short, freeriding is mountain biking at the fringe, and as such, it demands cutting-edge equipment and skills.

Gearing Up

Most freeride bikes boast 5 to 7 inches of suspension travel, powerful disc brakes, and hugely fat (as wide as 2.5-inch) tires with monstrous, dirt-munching knobs. A handful of diehards swing their legs over hardtail frames equipped with long-travel suspension forks, but most rely on the increased margin of error, control, and comfort afforded by a rear shock. There are literally dozens of freeride bikes on the market; choosing the right one for you is simply a matter of riding, riding, and riding some more. Most bike shops (well, the smart ones, anyway) aren't going to let you take a new freeride bike on a test spin over the terrain it's designed for—there's simply too great a risk of damage. But some shops rent freeride bikes, and if you hook up with a group of local riders, there should be plenty of opportunity to swing your leg over different bikes and get plenty of opinionated advice.

Another option is to modify your existing bike. Even if you have an old cross-country hardtail, you can realize dramatic changes in its handling over gnarly terrain simply by swapping out some key components.

Handlebar. If your bike is currently equipped with a flat handlebar, pull it off, and replace it with a riser bar that has at least an inch of upward sweep. This will effectively reduce the height difference between your saddle and your handlebar, making it much easier to get your butt behind the seat on hypersteep descents. It will also give you more leverage on the front end in tight, technical terrain. Oh, and it might just eliminate that nagging soreness in your lower back. Not bad for 30 to 50 bucks, eh?

Tires. Outfit your ride with the fattest set of tires that will fit, while still leaving enough space for mud clearance. On older cross-country bikes, you might not be able to go much wider than your current rubber. But if you can fit 2.1- or even 2.3-inch-wide tires, do it. You'll be amazed at the increase in traction, bump absorption, and overall stability and control.

Brakes. Many older frames are devoid of rear disc mounts. The secret is, that's okay. That's because almost all modern suspension forks are disc compatible, and since 80 percent of your braking power originates at the front brake, you can still realize huge benefits by replacing your front rim brake with a disc. Hydraulic models are best; they're also (of course) the most expensive. If you're just getting started and don't want to spend a ton of coin, slap on an inexpensive cable-actuated disc. You'll still be blown away by the increase in braking power and modulation.

Fork. If your suspension fork has less than 4 inches of travel and you're not racing, now's the time to upgrade. A good 4- or even 5-inch fork will dramatically change the way you ride. Don't go more than 5 inches, though, unless your bike was designed for it. That's because while the fork is built for big hits, your frame might not be; with the extra travel, you might be goaded into writing checks your frame can't cash. The result? You'll end up writing a real check . . . for a new frame. Also, the tall legs of a long-travel fork will raise the front end of your bike, which reduces the head angle and makes the steering less responsive. To a point, this is good thing (especially on fast downhills), but you don't want to take it too far, or you'll end up with slow, floppy steering that will make your bike hard to manage in technical terrain. In two words: not good.

Pedals. If you've been riding with clipless pedals, consider swapping them for old-school, large-platform flat pedals without toe clips. Sure, you'll lose some pedaling power, but you'll also gain the ability to instantly dab a foot on the ground should your freeriding antics go awry. Simply knowing you have this option will lend more confidence to your riding.

There you have it: Your budget freeride machine. Of course, there's only so much you can do by slapping parts on a bike that simply wasn't designed for the rigors of freeriding in the first place. It's a bit like putting race fuel in a moped. But you might be surprised by just how much difference it makes (the bike tweaks, not the race fuel); it's certainly enough to let you taste what all the hype's about. And given that good freeride bikes start at almost two grand, it's downright fiscally responsible!

But hold on. Think about it for a moment: What's the most important part of any ride? Hint: It's not on your bike. That's right, we're talking about you, about your flesh and bones and blood and grey matter. Of course, you already wear a helmet every time you hop on your bike, but the derring-do of freeriding demands something more than an ultralight cross-country helmet and a pair of spandex shorts, which offer a decent level of protection for buff singletrack but simply aren't gonna cut it when you're nosing your front wheel off a 10-foot cliff.

Here's what you need.

Full-face helmet

Motocross-style chest and back protector

Elbow/forearm pads

Knee/shin pads

Goggles

Full-finger gloves

Although there are plenty of cycling-specific manufacturers pumping out this sort of protective gear, you can save a few bucks by dipping into the gear closets of other sports. Motocross can provide the helmet, gloves, goggles, and chest protector, while hockey and soccer pads will help keep you in one piece while you get a feel for the sport. Once you're hooked, it's probably worth springing for bike-specific stuff, but in the meantime, remember that protective gear is nondiscriminatory. It'll save your butt no matter what you're doing.

Technique Tips for Aspiring Freeriders

Now that you're geared up, it's time to go throw yourself off the nearest cliff, right? Uh, sure. Just be certain your health insurance is paid up. And it might be a good idea to park a few paramedics at the bottom of the cliff. You know, for safety's sake.

Actually, there's a better idea: Read the rest of this chapter, which is loaded with tips from freeriding great **Richie Schley**. Schley, who lives in Whistler, BC, and runs freeride camps for all ages, is one of the original freeriders. He's been an innovator on the bike since the early '90s, and he shows no sign of slowing down. Even as younger riders emerge, Schley remains relevant and often shows up the youngsters at competitions and exhibitions around the world. He is, in short, the Michael Jordan of mountain biking. Here are his top five tips for achieving freeriding greatness. Or at least competence.

1. How to Survive Drops

Whether you're dropping off a 6-inch curb or a 6-foot rock, the technique, says Schley, is the same. In fact, Schley encourages new freeriders to think of all drops as simply a big curb. "The technique for riding drops is pretty simple," says Schley. "The problem is that people get freaked out by the height. So I tell my campers to always think about riding off a curb. Keep your speed steady, lean back, and let gravity do its thing. You don't want to pull up on the handlebar too much; instead, just lean back enough that your arms are nearly straight, but be sure to keep some bend in your elbows to help absorb landing shock." The other key, says Schley, is to land on your rear wheel first. "The flatter the landing, the sooner your rear wheel should touch down. If it's a steep downhill landing, your rear wheel should land just a moment before your front."

2. How to Catch Big Air

The allure of jumping is universal and timeless, and that's why you should add this skill to your freeriding repertoire. Jumping is more complicated than dropping, simply because you have the uphill transition of the jump to consider. Schley notes that many new riders on long-travel suspension bikes get themselves in trouble by approaching with too much speed, getting nervous, and slamming on the brakes just as they reach the jump. This causes their suspension to compress and then release as they leave the ground, turning their bike into a big spring and tossing them high into the air. The result? Carnage.

Instead, Schley recommends starting on small jumps that don't cause undue emotional distress. "Start slow enough that you won't feel nervous," says Schley. "Approach the jump with your arms loose and your eyes looking over the stem. As you leave the ground, gently pull the bike up toward your body and keep your eyes on your landing. Try to keep your weight centered over the bike." As with drops, you want your rear wheel to touch down first. If you don't believe this, try landing on your front wheel. On second thought, don't.

3. How to Ride Ladder Bridges

Nothing says "freeride" louder and clearer than the ladder bridge. In the forests of British Columbia, some ladder bridges run for hundreds of feet, twisting and turning and even incorporating other stunts, such as drops and teeter-totters.

Still, for the most part, ladder bridges demand more courage than skill. Think about it: If someone asked you to ride on flat ground within two lines a foot apart, you'd have no trouble. Heck, you might even throw in a wheelie or two. But when those two lines are elevated 10 feet above the ground, it's a whole new ballgame. It's all about conquering the fear. And not looking over the edge.

Schley recommends starting on flat ground, either riding along the painted stripe at the edge of the road or along the yellow painted portion of a sidewalk curb. "The key to learning ladder bridges is to ride the low stuff as if it were high, and the high stuff as if it were low," says Schley. In other words, when you're on the ground (or close to it), try to pretend you're 10 feet in the air and imagine that wavering from your chosen path will have serious repercussions. To keep from wavering, "always look at where you want to go, not where you don't," says Schley. Try to block everything from your mind and vision but the terrain that's immediately in front of your front wheel.

As you work your way onto higher bridges, maintain the same focus and remember that the actual riding doesn't demand great skill. The only real skill is to fool yourself into believing you're on the ground. If you can do that, you'll soon be a ladder bridge master.

4. How to Ride Steep Slopes

Like ladder bridges, steep slopes, whether they're made of rock or dirt, typically bark worse than they bite. In other words, they just aren't that difficult once you get your head around them. The trick, says Schley, is to drop in slowly, keeping your pedal level, maneuvering your butt well behind the saddle (Warning: You may get a bit of "butt burn" on the rear tire. Consider it a rite of passage), and feathering the brakes. If the transition out of the steep face is gradual, you can carry some speed, but if it ends abruptly, you need to proceed very slowly, or you'll do a nosedive when your front end hits the compression.

Proper braking technique is absolutely critical on steeps. Too many riders shy away from the front brake, afraid that it will send them hurtling over the handlebar. That won't happen, so long as you apply it slowly and don't do a "panic grab" on the brake lever. In fact, in many cases, it's the rear brake you should be cautious with because of its tendency to lock the rear wheel, which can send you into an out-of-control skid. Again, your best and safest bet is to practice on shorter, less-steep slopes, getting a feel for the body position and braking technique.

5. How to Fly through Corners at Warp Speed

Watching a top freerider flow through a corner is like watching poetry in motion. It seems as if they hardly touch the brakes, and while most of us have to sprint like a bloodhound to regain the speed we lost, they rocket out of the turn. How do they do it? According to Schley, it's all about body language.

First, you've got to look ahead. "The slower and sharper the corner, the more important it is to lead with your head," says Schley. "Stick it out in front of your body a bit and keep your eyes locked on the exit of the corner. Everything your body and bike do will follow what you do with your head."

Schley has another critical piece of instruction: Keep your pedals level. This is harder than it sounds; most riders tend to drop the outside pedal in fast corners. But Schley insists that level pedals—at three and nine o'clock, respectively—provide better traction and improve reaction time. "When all your weight is on your outside pedal, it's almost impossible to keep your body in line with your lean angle," explains Schley. "Although it feels more stable at first, you're actually putting yourself at greater risk of losing traction and sliding your tires. If you keep your pedals level, your weight will automatically be centered over your bike side-to-side, and you'll have much more traction and control. Plus, you'll be able to pick up speed much more quickly coming out of the corner."

There you have it. The basics of freeriding, as told by the discipline's master. But that's not all: Schley understands that freeriding demands more than solid technique. To that end, we asked him to dish up some of his best off-the-bike tips. Read on; you might find a surprise or two.

Get tough. "You are going to feel like everyone on the mountain is better and cooler than you. Heck, some of them might even tell you they are. Don't let them get you down; just concentrate on your own game and pretty soon you'll be doing the same stuff they are."

Gear up. "If you don't pad up and protect yourself, you won't get far. Unless it's by ambulance." (See? We told you so.)

Have faith in your equipment. "If you have a sick bike with 6 to 8 inches of travel, you should be able to land almost anything. Don't blame your equipment; instead, spend your energy working on your skills."

Embrace the shuttle. "If you shuttle, you'll get way more descending and your skills will soar. Don't stop riding uphill, though: You'll get too chubby to put your armor on."

Take one of my clinics. "Do you really think you know everything? Of course not. I, on the other hand, do."

Ride with people who are better than you. "It's the best way to learn, but make sure to be the best on the ride sometimes, 'cause you will need the confidence boost."

Don't die wondering. "If you don't take chances, you won't know the outcome."

18 »»»

24 HOURS OF POWER

Back in 1992, the first 24 Hours of Canaan mountain bike race was held in Canaan, West Virginia. Hosted by a forward-thinking race promoter named Laird Knight, the event drew a handful of intrepid mountain bikers who thought that racing through the night sounded like good fun.

No one—not even Knight—could have guessed just how popular 24-hour mountain bike racing would become. These days, big 24-hour events draw literally thousands of racers, attracted to the team aspect (most 24-hour racers compete as part of a five-person relay team) and the festival-like atmosphere, which, despite the grueling athletic demands of the genre, is rife with keg beer, grilled hot dogs, and blaring rock music. At 24-hour races, there seems to be a strange juxtaposition at work: Although these events are perhaps the most physically daunting of any mountain bike racing format, the attitude is the least serious and most welcoming.

Which is not to say you needn't prepare. A growing handful of twisted individuals choose to enter these events solo, but even if you go the team route (and for your first 24-hour event, don't even think of anything else), you're going to need to undertake some specific training. Don't worry; we're not going to get all scientific and wonky on you (in fact, just forget we mentioned the "T" word at all). What we are going to do, with the help of Trek/VW's multitime 24-hour solo world champ **Chris Eatough**, is give you the tools you need to get the most out of the experience.

Sleepless on Singletrack

"For most casual racers, a 24-hour team race is like three or four regular cross-country races with a few hours' rest in between," says Eatough. "One of the best ways to prepare for this is to ride 'two-a-days': two rides in a single day." Daunting as that sounds, Eatough suggests it needn't take over your life. "On a regular workday, try to ride at least an hour in the morning and a slightly longer ride, maybe an hour and a half or 2 hours, in the evening. Commuting is a great way to make this happen." Remember, you don't want to do two-a-days every day; once or twice a week is plenty. The idea is to get your body accustomed to repeated efforts on the bike within a relatively short period of time.

No matter how many two-a-days you do, you can't forgo bread-and-butter endurance rides, says Eatough. "Even though the laps in a 24-hour race may only be around an hour, the fatigue is cumulative, which makes these events a huge test of endurance. That's why you've gotta test yourself with long rides, preferably off-road so you learn how to handle your bike when you're really tired." Eatough recommends working up to 5 hours, time permitting. "Use these rides to make yourself aware of what kind of food works for you while exercising, which shorts and saddles feel best, and what bike setup you like."

While long days in the saddle are critical, so too are shorter, more intense efforts, which will prepare you for the speed of racing. At least once a week, Eatough recommends a short (1- to 2-hour) ride with multiple hard efforts of at least 5 minutes each. Start with three of these efforts, and work your way up to six to eight, allowing for complete recovery in between.

As race day (and night) approaches, it's tempting to ratchet up the training. Bad idea, says Eatough. "Avoid any strenuous training the week leading up to the race. There's nothing you can do at this point to build fitness; any hard efforts will just make you tired, without enough time to recover for the race. Instead, stay loose and focused with short rides, including steady riding with just a few short efforts to keep your legs spinning over."

With your body attended to, it's time to take a look at your equipment. If you think 'round-the-clock racing is tough on your body, wait until you see what it does to your bike. "The most important element is that your equipment is tested and reliable," says Eatough. "You need to train on the same setup you're going to race on to ensure that you'll be comfortable on the bike and confident that you can deal with any mechanical issues that crop up. Pay particular attention to your wheels, tires, and drivetrain. Make sure these parts are in good condition going into the race and if it's possible, have spares on hand."

Eatough is bullish on full suspension for 24-hour racing. "If the course is very smooth, a hardtail might be okay, but for almost all conditions, a cross-country full-suspension bike with 3 to 4 inches of travel is better," says the champ, who races on a tricked-out full-suspension Trek that weighs less than 25 pounds. "Full suspension will help reduce fatigue and keep you strong throughout the race. It's amazing how much difference it makes as the race wears on." Eatough also recommends two more pieces of modern mountain-biking technology: disc brakes and tubeless wheels and tires. "Discs just have so much more power and are so much better in adverse conditions," says Eatough. "And with tubeless tires, you can run slightly lower pressure for better traction and more comfort and control. Plus, there's less chance of suffering a flat tire. Believe me, you really don't want to have to change a tube at three in the morning in the pouring rain."

Another absolutely critical element is your light setup. "The best setup is a handlebar light with the battery attached to the frame or water bottle cage, and a helmet light with the battery in your back pocket or hydration pack. If you have powerful lights, your vision of the trail at night should be almost as good as during the day, and having two lights prevents a failure from leaving you completely in the dark," says Eatough, who recommends HID (High Intensity Discharge) models, which are pricey but put out almost twice as much light. No matter what light you use, it's important to test it thoroughly before the big event. "Test your lights with a few night rides to find out the best angles and mounting," suggests Eatough. "The lights should focus close to the rider on slow trails (about 6 to 12 feet in front), and further away for fast trails (12 to 40 feet). Also test your lights' burn and recharge times beforehand to make sure you will have juice for each of your night laps." Most race organizers provide charging stations for extra batteries, but be sure to ask, lest you be left in the dark.

Next up: clothing. Don't be seduced by warm summer days, says Eatough. "Even in July and August, it can get really cold at night. It's important to stay warm, especially right before and after your laps. Use a large jacket that you can take off quickly at the start line just before your lap. The best are the kind that come down to your knees, with snap buttons in the front, like football players sometimes wear on the sidelines."

The remainder of your riding apparel can probably come straight from your current stock. Bring at least two pairs of shorts (the more the better, especially if it's raining or muddy); tights or knee warmers; a jersey or two; arm warmers; and a light, water- and wind-resistant jacket to stuff in your jersey pocket. Gloves are critical, and you'll want at least two pairs of eyewear—one with shaded lenses for day use, and one with clear lenses for night laps. For downtime, bring loose, comfy workout clothes that will keep you warm and dry.

"Organization is really important," says Eatough. "Have a clean pair of shorts and racing jersey ready for each lap, and keep your other clothing and equipment orderly and on hand so as to save time, energy, and stress before and after laps. It's also easy to mix up clothing and equipment with teammates, so put your name on everything and—stay organized."

Eatough also recommends packing as much emergency gear as possible. "If you don't have access to a spare bike, take spare tires, tubes, spokes, a chain, rear derailleur, CO_2 cartridges, grips, and a saddle. Take all your bike tools, as well as fix-all staples like duct tape, zip-ties, superglue, safety pins, and bungee cords. You never know what you're going to have to fix out there."

At the Race

You're geared up, well rested, and ready to charge. Excellent. But have you thought about tactics? Racing around the clock, on a team with four other people, demands a bit more thought than simply charging out of the gate and going until you collapse (though it may not feel much different at times).

One thing to remember, says Eatough, is to keep a lid on your efforts. "The intensity should be similar to a regular cross-country race, but try to avoid sudden surges and all-out efforts, which really take a toll. Try to get into a groove and stay there. Remember, these are long races, so don't get sucked into a dogfight on the first lap." Another factor is peer pressure. "The desire to perform for your teammates can be a strong motivator, but it can backfire later on in the race if you don't recover," explains Eatough. "Try to maintain some reserves so you can really impress them with a fast lap at seven in the morning."

Eatough also recommends bringing a stationary trainer. "A short warmup before your laps will make a huge difference. Shoot for 10 minutes of easy spinning, followed by a gradual 2-minute increase in intensity up to about 80 percent of your max."

There are few rules about how to best utilize your team members' specific strengths and weaknesses, but there is one cardinal sin of 24-hour racing: missing a transition (when one rider comes in and the next goes out). "Always expect your teammate to pull the fastest lap of the race and even then, be a few minutes early to the transition area," says Eatough. "It helps if you can have a friend work as a 'spotter' by standing a couple of minutes before the finish line, and signaling or radio alerting when your rider comes by so the next rider has a warning." One more tactical tip from the master: "If you are in a close race, you might be able to get an edge by having your strongest riders race more laps toward the end of the race."

Eating for the Long Haul

Of course, the best laid plans will come to naught if you don't keep your body adequately fueled and hydrated. Since you've experimented with different foods and fluids during training (and you have, right?), by now you have a good idea what works for you and what leaves your stomach churning. But due to the unique demands of 24-hour races, it's a good idea to pack a wide variety of food: A 24-hour racer at four in the morning is like a pregnant woman. Strange cravings are the norm, and if you don't have that tin of smoked oysters, you can't very well eat that tin of smoked oysters, now, can you?

No matter what you crave, "it's important to stay ahead of your calorie and hydration needs," says Eatough, who recommends noshing a small snack as soon as you finish each lap and then eating a larger portion once you're clean and comfortable. "And drink water or sports drink pretty much constantly," says Eatough. "It's really tough to keep up on the hydration aspect." Off the bike, Eatough likes to fill his stomach with fairly bland, high-carbohydrate food like bagels, pasta, bananas, oranges, potatoes, soup, and hot tea. On the bike, he munches on energy bars and gels between sips from his hydration pack. When he feels his blood sugar lagging, Eatough reaches into his bag of tricks and pulls out soda, energy gels, and cookies.

Finally, says Eatough, remember to keep in the spirit of the sport and have fun. "Very few teams are racing to win. That's what makes 24-hour racing so cool. Everyone's just out there having a good time. Sure, they're hurting, but that's just part of the fun."

TRAIL MIX

On technical sections, steep climbs, and curvy trails, your butt should float just above the saddle. Keep contact with it, but don't put much weight there. This lets you shift your weight more quickly and easily and allows you to put pressure against either side of the saddle to help control the bike's side-to-side movement.

If your rear wheel skids on a descent, use more front brake. A skid means that your wheel has lost most of its power to slow and control the bike.

Start long climbs in a gear that feels too easy. Believe us, by the time you get to the top, it won't feel too easy anymore. But you'll be doing a whole lot better than the folks who charged the bottom and blew up at the halfway point.

When you bunny-hop, concentrate on throwing your bike forward as well as up. This is how you get distance.

Look through riders ahead of you. People move around a lot when they're mountain biking, so most of the time, you can get a decent (although shifting) line of sight—enough to anticipate the trail.

When you get comfortable riding at high speed, you'll be super-confident at 90 percent of that speed. That's why many pro downhillers train on motocross bikes. Or maybe it's just a handy excuse to twist some throttle.

Think of braking as a process. It begins not with a lever squeeze, but with a weight shift. Rise off the saddle and extend your arms while keeping some bend in your elbows. This keeps your weight off the front wheel. The result is a more controlled bike.

Ride against the same guys every week in order to build up ongoing competitive steam that makes you all better riders.

If you're having trouble riding smoothly over rough terrain, think about keeping your bike quiet. The clanging and clanking you hear as you stutter through rocks and roots is your sign that you could be riding smoother, faster, and with more control. Practice riding with your ears open.

➤ In a section of small rollers or stutter bumps, shift onto the middle or big ring. The resultant lower cadence "smoothes out" the bumps so that you don't feel as much shock as you pedal.

➤ Shadowing a better rider is a great way to learn new moves. You see techniques and copy them without thinking, which improves your confidence and understanding of what's possible.

➤ Being too cautious only makes trail riding more difficult. Beginners tend to slow down for everything that looks threatening, and their lack of momentum results in dabs, falls, and frustration. You need some speed to help your wheels carry through stuff that wants to stop them or change their direction.

➤ Try riding at night to develop a new set of reflexes and intuitive skills. A trail you've ridden a hundred times becomes a new experience after the sun sets.

➤ To do a good wheelie, don't forget the "second pull." Compress the front wheel, then lift it smoothly by bending your elbows, shifting your weight back, and pulling back and up on the handlebar. Then do a second pull—lift the bar higher with another elbow bend.

➤ A seatbag full of tools is cool, but when you go on long trips, take a larger tool bag or pack your hydration pack with another spare tube and patches, a bottle of lube, a small floor pump, a pedal wrench, a small crescent wrench, brake and derailleur cables, zip-ties, and assorted bolts that fit things like cleats and brake arms. You might not need the bag very often, but when you do need it, it'll be a trip saver.

➤ A major cause of poor brake performance is pad residue on the rims. Buff it off with steel wool, fine sandpaper, or emery paper. If you have disc brakes, get in the habit of checking your pads for wear: Because they're hiding out inside the rotors, it's easy to forget about them.

On twisty courses where you can't see the next bend, be extra careful. Ride with one finger of each hand on the brake levers, ready for action.

Whether you have clipless pedals or toeclips with straps, practice getting each foot out during different parts of the pedal stroke. When you're riding, you won't always have the luxury of freeing your favorite foot when the pedal is at the bottom of the stroke (the most natural and common position for releasing). Learn to extract each foot in all positions, and you'll save yourself a few bruises.

Find the halfway-down point of a hill. Start at the top, ride to that mark, then try to come to a stop as quickly as you can beyond that mark without locking the brakes or skidding. This will help you hone your emergency braking skills. Just don't kill yourself. Heck, don't even hurt yourself, okay?

A faster bike is a more stable bike. It's called inertia. Make it work for you.

To dry your cycling shorts fast, roll them in a towel after they've been washed. Stand on one end of the towel and wring it as tight as you can with both hands, then hang up the shorts. They should be completely dry in just a few hours.

You yank. You heave. You jerk your handlebar up and back for all you're worth, but that dang front wheel stays glued to the dirt. So why can't you wheelie? Most likely your arms are too stiff (unlock those elbows) or you have too much of your upper-body weight forward. In any case, take this cure-all advice and try again in the morning. Shift to one of your three easiest gears, then time your pedal strokes so that one of your feet begins going down just as you try to lift the bar. Really mash down the pedal, and say, "Whoa, Trigger!" No luck? Try, "Heigh-ho, Silver!" You should at least develop a teeny wheelie with this technique.

If you can rock your helmet off your head forward or backward, it's not fitted properly. The front and back straps should join just under your ear. The chin strap should be tight enough so that you can just feel it when you swallow.

▶▶ If you see chainring marks on the top of a log, don't move it. Someone can ride it, or at least is trying to. Ride the mountain instead of making the mountain rideable.

▶▶ Ride your favorite trail in the opposite direction. You won't believe how different it seems. Just don't crash into yourself coming the other way.

▶▶ To make grease and gunk slide right off your chain, do the following before washing your bike: Spray degreaser on the chain, then put three or four drops of liquid dishwashing soap on a sponge. Hold the sponge around the chain while you backpedal three or four times. When you hose down the bike, the chain will clean itself.

▶▶ If you're on rocks or an unstable or slippery surface, you need to let go of the brakes until you reach a better place to apply them. This means that sometimes you have to go faster than you'd like—one of the toughest things to learn about riding technical sections.

▶▶ To stop the handlebar from cutting through the grips in a crash, slip a nickel into the end of each grip when you install them.

▶▶ To make cleanup easier, hose down your bike as soon as possible after a gunky ride. Once muck dries on your bike, it doubles or triples your maintenance time. Spray those lovely legs of yours while you're at it. Only posers walk around with caked calves 3 hours after a ride ends.

▶▶ In a suspension fork or rear shock, preload is the amount of spring tension. Too much preload makes a fork stiff and keeps it from absorbing small, frequent bumps. Too little preload allows your body weight to sink the fork, which robs it of much of its ability to compress and limits how well it can absorb bumps.

▶▶ Don't ease off your pedaling as you reach a summit. Sure, you're tired, but maintain your cadence, shift up to a bigger gear, and roll away. Most riders slack off even before they quite reach the crest, so this is a good way to gain time and hurt friends, which is even more fun than it sounds.

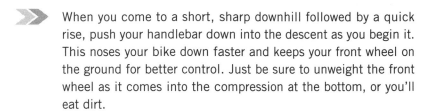 When you come to a short, sharp downhill followed by a quick rise, push your handlebar down into the descent as you begin it. This noses your bike down faster and keeps your front wheel on the ground for better control. Just be sure to unweight the front wheel as it comes into the compression at the bottom, or you'll eat dirt.

If you want to smooth out your line, stop focusing on small objects and parts of the trail. By concentrating on only the biggest obstacles and features, your body will stop overreacting to twigs, rocks, small changes in the angle of the trail surface, and other unimportant stuff.

Lube your chain at least 30 minutes before you begin a ride. Let the lube soak in, then wipe the chain well just before you start out. This allows the lube to penetrate the links, but doesn't leave much on the outside of the chain where it attracts dirt. Remember that too much lube is as bad, if not worse, than too little lube. Put too much on, and you'll end up with a gunked-up (yes, that's a technical term) drivetrain.

If you have a roof rack, you can easily dry soaked shoes after a ride. Just securely click the shoes into your pedals before mounting the bike on the roof. The rushing air does a splendid job. No roof rack? Stuff your shoes with newspaper, which will absorb much of the excess moisture.

After a rainy ride, remove your seatpost and turn your bike upside down. It's scary how much water will drain out.

If you've just gotten a suspension bike, make sure to bring your shock pump along on the first few rides. And use it! It's amazing how much your new bike's personality will change with just a few strokes of the shock.

Because climbing is a repetitive act, it helps to think repetitive things. Try repeating a phrase over and over, something simple like, "I'll make it" or "It's only rock and roll but I like it." This gives you a rhythm and keeps you from dwelling on the effort you're making.

Get bonus traction on technical climbs by standing and lifting your front wheel over large rocks and ledges, then jerking the back wheel onto them and using these harder surfaces for a better grip.

When you're climbing out of the saddle, be sure to scoop your feet back at the bottom of each stroke. This will eliminate a big dead spot in your power transmission and you'll climb faster.

Don't always go out for a ride. Sometimes go out to practice. Ride to tough trail sections and repeat them three or four times, trying new techniques on each pass. Don't spend so much time on one that you get frustrated. Move on to the next challenge.

If your riding skills seem to be improving too slowly, your problem is most likely shabby fitness. Anyone can learn the techniques that good mountain bikers need, but some people don't have the strength and endurance to consistently enact them. Concentrate on building an aerobic base with long, steady rides—at least three per week for 2 months. You'll see an amazing improvement in your ability to pull off bike-handling moves.

The key to smooth, reliable, nondamaging gear changes when you're pushing hard is to ease your pedal pressure at the instant you move the shift lever. You need to lighten the load on the chain for about one revolution so it won't balk, crunch, or possibly break. Then hit the gas again.

Your brakes aren't for stopping. They're for controlling your speed.

Ride as close as possible to people who are better than you. Don't just ride with them; stay close and study what they do.

Rocks under water give better traction than those partially submerged, which are more likely to be mossy or slick.

Lift your front wheel just before you drop off a shelf, and you'll land on both wheels at once, or on the back wheel first. Either way is smoother and safer than landing on your front wheel first.

⟫ Next time you remove your wheels for any kind of maintenance, scrub your brake pads with medium-grit sandpaper to abrade the surface, remove caked-on grit, and improve braking power.

⟫ The easiest way to find your maximum heart rate is to subtract your age from 220. That's fine if you're lazy or don't care about accuracy.

⟫ The best way to find your max heart rate is with a medically supervised stress test or max VO_2 test at a hospital or sports medicine facility.

⟫ The do-it-yourself way—after obtaining your doctor's approval—is to ride your bike to a long, steep hill. Be sure you're well rested. Wear a heart-rate monitor, preferably one that stores the highest pulse you reach. After warming up, start the climb and steadily increase your effort to the point where you can't go any harder. Then go harder. And even harder than that. Sprint! The heart rate you see through those black spots is your max. You can use that figure to accurately calculate your training ranges.

19 ⟫⟫

GO WITH THE FLOW

Watch any mountain bike race (or ride along with your local trail aces) and you'll soon be amazed at how some riders glide over terrain while others blithely blunder along, bouncing their front wheels off rocks and desperately trying to muscle their bikes. Good mountain bikers seem to levitate. They flow along a trail like—you knew this was coming—water down a streambed. It's magic.

Before some intermediate techniques are introduced, it may be helpful to review the basics of how good riders perform this sleight-of-wheel. They're simply tapping into the flow. This isn't so much a physical skill as a mind-set. That's why how-to descriptions often turn mushy—it's easier to teach a concrete technique with repeatable skills than something rising out of the mind-body connection.

But some mountain bikers, like **Tom Masterson**, a multitime national champion who now runs mountain bike camps in Fairlee, Vermont, can get these abstract ideas across. These steps used by Masterson will get you—and your juices—flowing on every ride.

A Is for Anticipate

You know by now that your body tends to move in the direction your eyes are focused. Stare doggedly only a few feet ahead of your front wheel, and you'll have to make split-second decisions to avoid obstacles. Everything comes at you so fast, you have time only to react, not anticipate.

But if you make a habit of scanning 20 to 30 feet up the trail, you'll ride smoothly, without the tension and fatigue that ruin flow. Pretend that you have two sets of eyes. One pair sees the big picture, helping you pick the best line through obstacles. The other pair detects all the trail's subtle detail so you can make tiny adjustments along the way. Concentrate mostly on your big-picture focus by looking well ahead of your bike. Trust your peripheral vision to avoid rocks and roots. If you keep your head up and most of your attention focused down the trail, your bike will flow along the line of your gaze.

Looking down the trail lets you anticipate gearing changes, too. If you're scanning ahead when you approach a rock-littered uphill section, you can shift down and spin through. Many riders don't get into a lower gear soon enough, so they get stuck, trying to power through the rubble in a cog that's several teeth too little. Then again, you should shift to the middle or large chainring ahead of time for downhills. This will reduce the slack that can cause the chain to slap the frame or jump off the front chainrings. It will also keep you from spinning uselessly in too low a gear when you need to apply power.

B Is for Balance

Flow depends mightily on balance—a feel for where your weight is on the bike—particularly on steep climbs. If your balance is poor, you'll be forced into quick, jerky steering adjustments leading to a squirrelly front wheel.

Try to be like a cat. When felines are poised to pounce, they're loose, not rigid. Practice catlike balance when rolling slowly along on a grassy surface. Get on all fours—your weight on your hands and feet and your butt off the saddle. Then pounce by jumping the bike from your balanced position. There's no need to get big air. Just get both wheels a couple of inches off the ground, roll ahead a few feet, and repeat. Relax.

As you improve, go slower. Soon, you'll be hopping in one spot and you'll have developed the balance needed to flow along the trail. Your bike is not merely a machine—it's your direct connection to the trail.

C Is for Calm

A relaxed body creates a relaxed mind. If your handgrip is loose and your shoulders are flexible, your nature can become calm, ready for anything the trail throws at you. Avoid the panicked response as you look ahead. Instead, think, "I can help my bike get over this obstacle."

Here's how to practice. Find a section of trail with an obstacle, like a rock ledge, that you're having trouble riding over. It should be something you clear only half the time—the sort of challenge that makes you tense up when you spot it looming around the corner. Take a couple of deep breaths and ride it slowly so you can work on timing. It's easy to relax because at such a slow speed, you can just put a foot down if you need to. As you get better, increase your speed a little, but don't lose that feeling of calm. Before you know it, you'll be flowing over that ledge.

Being calm also means being light on the bike. Here's an analogy: When you get tired while hiking, you begin to plod along. Your feet feel heavy, almost attached to the ground. But if you concentrate on a springy stride and don't let your feet stay in contact with the ground for long, you'll bounce up the trail. It's the same way on a bike. A tense upper body makes your bike feel 10 pounds heavier. So ride light—and levitate.

RIDE A NARROW TRAIL

Watching new mountain bikers on their first singletrack rides is a great reminder of what a miracle it is to stay on that type of trail. As a novice, you just can't pin the trail under your wheels—the darn thing keeps slithering out from under you. Experienced riders glide along securely and speedily as if on monorails, jabbering about techniques like rolling over logs or scaling unexpected humps, while your entire focus is aimed at simply maintaining some sort of contact with the trail. You crash into bushes, crawl through grass, and drop into depressions. You broadside rocks and sideswipe branches.

Don't worry. You're not hopeless. Everyone rides like this at first—and everyone gets over it. Some of the solution is more acclimation. Eventually your head will get used to being on singletrack and it will calm down. But there are things you can do to get through the initiation more quickly. If riding on wide stuff is easy but narrow trails are stopping you from advancing your skills, try these solutions.

Loosen your elbows. Controlled mountain biking depends on loose elbows and knees acting as shock absorbers. This is true even on suspension bikes, so don't think you're off the hook just because you dropped the long dollar on mechanical shocks. Start paying attention in situations that might normally make you freeze—like a twisty trail about a foot wide. If your elbows are stiff, your handlebar will jerk every time your brain flinches at something in the trail. Stiff arms magnify small movements into big jitters.

Stop looking at everything. Even on a smooth trail, novices dart their vision from one edge to the other, the trees at the side, a rock, a small dip—whatever isn't smooth ground. A technical trail that is littered with roots, rocks, and jagged ups and downs is an exercise in sensory overload.

You don't need to look at everything. Your subconscious and your peripheral vision will see it all. Take the pressure off the aware part of yourself and concentrate on only one thing: the path you want your bike to take. This comes right back to the most fundamental principle of bike riding: Where you stare, you will steer.

Fight the panic. Long after staying on the trail is simple reflex, the tightrope syndrome will occasionally return to ruin your life. Even experienced riders can revert to awkward wobbles when confronted with sidehill paths. (This is when the trail cuts across the hill or mountain, creating a steep drop-off on one side. It's probably the toughest type of singletrack for beginners to ride.) The basic technique for riding well in this situation is not to panic—keep your eyes on where you want to go instead of glancing into the "abyss of death." This takes willpower and concentration. You can do it. Condition your brain as well as your body to follow your vision.

Lean with care. On a sidehill trail, your instinct will be to lean your bike away from the drop—into the hill where you'll be safer if you fall. But this is bad for two reasons: It puts your inside pedal closer to the upside, making you more likely to clip the ground and lose your balance, and it slants your tires outward, just the way you don't want to make a slip. So either lean your bike slightly toward the drop (so your body won't slant that way) or keep both your bike and your body vertical.

Maintain straight speed. Everyone has a speed at which the bike stops stuttering and settles into a smooth, straight-ahead line. Find that speed. That's how fast you should go when you're crossing narrow stuff. Slower isn't safer. Neither is faster.

Be decisive on the approach. When you're coming to a bridge or section of sidehill singletrack, make a go or no-go decision before you reach the scary narrow part. Decisiveness is steadiness. Indecision and mental hiccups are wobbles. Aim for a smooth, controlled entry, but don't panic if it doesn't happen. Keep looking ahead at how much room there is for your wheels. Don't look down at how far you'll fall or how close your knobs are to one edge. And always remember: There is no shame in walking. The challenge will still be there the next time through, when you're having a more confident day.

21 »»»

BUNNY-HOPPING

What's the point of learning to bunny-hop?" asks the rider. "With the kind of biking I do, I'll never need to get big air." He squeezes the brakes, jerks the front wheel off the ground, and lurches forward clumsily to clear another 6-inch log. "I'd rather be solid than flashy," he says.

That's when he gets the bunny-hopping-is-like-life lecture. At one end of the spectrum is the flying, thumb-your-nose-at-gravity extreme high jump reserved for licensed pilots. But at the other end is an easy, useful sort of everyday levitation. If you learn to hop over small obstacles, you'll have an easier time entering "the flow"—the smooth, fluid groove of good mountain biking. Here's a simple, step-by-step guide to low-level aeronautics.

1. Get off your bike and jump as high as you can. Try it with bent knees first, then without bending your knees at all. It's much easier to touch the sky if you crouch down first, isn't it? The same is true when you want to bunny-hop your bike—bend your knees first and you'll go much higher.

2. Get on your bike and pedal slowly. Lift the front wheel about 6 inches off the ground by pulling up with your arms as you shift

your weight slightly back from your hips. Coordinate the upward pull of your arms with a downward push on the forward pedal. The hard pedal stroke lightens the front end and makes it easier to lift. Coordination is more important than strength, so practice lifting the wheel over a line scratched in the dirt to nail the timing.

3. Next, learn to lift the bike's back end. At slow speed, keep your crankarms horizontal and pull your heels up as you shift your weight slightly to the front. Again, use a line on the ground to work on timing. (Hint: It's much easier if your feet are firmly attached with clipless pedals.) Don't go hog-wild—you're just learning to unweight the rear wheel.

4. Put the two moves together. Begin by rolling along slowly and hopping the bike up and down. Remember to bend your knees and elbows, push the bike into the ground to compress the tires, and spring up—all in one fluid motion. Immediately lift the front wheel, like a plane lifting the nose before the main gear follows, then bring up the rear. Don't just think "up"—also think "forward," like the arc of a diver off a springboard.

5. Take your new skill out on the trail. Try hopping over sticks or small rocks until your confidence grows. And remember: Crouch down first. Bend those knees and elbows so you can spring up like a cat. Think "up and forward." Project your

landing on the other side of the obstacle. Timing is everything. Practice until your bunny-hop is automatic. When you come around a corner on the trail and see a log across the way, you'll fly over it without thinking about technique at all.

THE TRIPOD TURN

Bicycles can be unstable machines, so sometimes you need to help prop them up in corners with a quick dab of your foot. Now, if you have any memory whatsoever, you probably remember freeriding legend Richie Schley talking about keeping your feet clipped in and level through corners.

Schley wasn't wrong: That is the ideal way to corner. But out in the real world of roots and rocks and rain and sand and whatnot, things aren't always ideal. Sometimes, you need a "crutch" in the form of an extended leg. This is especially true when you're pushing the pace on a section of trail you're not familiar with.

This technique rarely involves dragging your foot through turns like a dirt-track motorcycle racer. Your foot shouldn't actually contact the ground unless you lose balance or start to slide out. The idea is to have your foot ready to touch just in case.

The Technique

1. First, get ready for the corner. Brake early when you're still going in a straight line and both feet are in the pedals. You have more control when your feet are clipped in, so release your foot only after you've slowed.

2. Put the outside pedal down and stand on it, with your butt an inch or so off the saddle. Weight the outside pedal hard. This drives the tires into the ground for better cornering traction.

3. Unclip your inside foot and extend it a bit forward of your center of gravity. Think of aiming your foot into the turn. Some riders keep their extended leg straight, others let it dangle. Try keeping yours slightly bent so your foot hovers above the ground. If you start to drift, you can correct with a quick dab.

4. As soon as you begin exiting the turn, clip back in.

The tripod technique works best on rounded corners when you're coming in fast. If you need to pedal out of the corner immediately, such as when the exit is uphill, keep both feet clipped in so you can accelerate faster.

Some riders like to unclip when descending tight switchbacks, but that can be a mistake. Good switchback technique involves getting your weight back behind the saddle, which is tough to do with one foot out. If you unclip, you may get caught in front of the seat and end up doing a one-legged hop around the switchback while sitting on the top tube. That's not very efficient or comfy. Practice switchbacks with both feet clipped in.

Be ready to touch your foot to prevent sliding out.

Finally, what do you do with your upper body while tripod turning? There's usually no need to get fancy, at least not consciously. Just think about keeping your weight balanced between your hands on the bar and the outside foot on the pedal. This makes it easier to do the subtle forward and backward weight shifts necessary to keep the tires from skidding out.

23 »»»

UPHILL SKILLS

Y ou probably judge your climbing prowess on how fast you ascend—which of your riding friends you can keep up with or which ones you leave behind. That's a fair way to rate yourself, but you won't improve much if you only think about climbing faster. The quality you need to develop isn't speed, it's power, which will translate to speed. Power means many things: having the oomph to overcome obstacles when you're already expending energy to climb, sustaining a burst needed to scale a steep section, or maintaining your pace throughout a long ascent.

When you think of climbing in these terms, you can see that your opponent isn't the speedometer, but your own energy supply. Use the following tips to conserve your power and convert what you have into faster climbs.

Stay in your seat. Standing on hills burns more energy because your body must support itself as well as propel the bike. Standing is great for juking over obstacles, using different muscles, stretching on long climbs, or hammering short sections, but most of your climbing should be done from the saddle. There's no rule dictating how much standing is too much, but, in general, the heavier you are, the more you should be sitting on climbs.

Drop your nose. As the ground tilts up, you should lean down toward the handlebar. This helps you maintain traction while still delivering peak power to the pedals. Many riders try to retain traction by scooting forward on the seat. It's better to lean your chest toward the stem. The steeper the rise, the lower the lean.

Ride relaxed and steady. Stay loose to save energy, absorb jolts easier, and have more control in technical sections. The upper body is the key, but concentrate on your hands and jaws. If these are loose, your back, shoulders, and neck will be, too. Even in technical terrain, your grip should be relaxed but firm. Don't clench the bar: no white knuckles. On a smooth climb, try drumming your fingers as a reminder. Also try to minimize your upper body's side-to-side movement. Swaying or bobbing helps establish a rhythm, but it has to be natural. Don't force it or overdo it.

Breathe like a machine. Instead of mindless panting, develop a solid, rhythmic breathing pattern that you can synchronize with your pedal strokes. This helps you maintain a steady pace and keeps you from feeling out of control (and psyching yourself out) during extreme efforts. Steady breaths deliver oxygen better than even the fastest gasps, especially if you actively force air from your lungs instead of just passively exhaling. This flushes more carbon dioxide (the main cause of shortness of breath) out of your bloodstream.

Spin instead of mash. One of the most common mistakes is climbing with slow pedal strokes in hard gears. Not only does this style waste energy and blast your heart rate over the top, but it also makes you more likely to blow out a knee. Your most efficient cadence is probably between 70 and 90 rpm. Whenever possible, climb in a gear that lets you maintain this rate. Pay attention to how you pedal. Apply even pressure all the way around your strokes, pulling back through the bottom and pushing across the top to make them as smooth and round as possible.

Ride with your head. These three simple tricks pay off big.

1. On uphill curves, take the outside line. It's longer, but it's almost always shallower and easier.

2. Don't zigzag. It might feel easier to cut back and forth while climbing, but computers and smart people have proven that weaving takes more energy than riding straight.

3. Bungee up. Pick a tree, big rock, or other object way up the climb. Throw a "mental bungee cord" around the object, then pull yourself up to it. When you get there, toss your bungee around another anchor farther up the hill. It's a great mind game to get you up an intolerable climb.

Use different muscles. The more upright you sit on a climb, the more you use your thighs. As you bend toward the handlebar, your buttocks muscles begin to deliver more power. It's easy to become so zoned on long climbs that you forget to vary your riding position and completely wipe out one group of muscles instead of sharing the effort.

Use bar ends more. Not all bikes have these handlebar extensions. If yours does, train yourself to use them more often. Many riders grip their bar ends only when they stand to climb and want to rock the bike from side to side. But you can benefit from them even when you sit. Slide your hands onto the joint of the bar ends and handlebar, or just slightly higher up on the bar ends. This wider position opens your chest and helps you breathe easier, stretches your hands slightly to relieve cramps and aches, and subtly changes your riding position—all of which makes you more comfortable when you climb. The better you feel, the stronger you ride.

Climbing the Wall

As just mentioned, simply by leaning farther forward (dropping your nose toward the stem) or sitting more upright, you can shift your weight fore or aft. The alternative is to actually move forward or backward by sliding on the saddle, which is less efficient and unwieldy.

But as cool as a subtle weight shift is, it won't work for really steep climbs. On ascents that are almost too steep to walk up, your rear tire will spin out no matter how low and forward you lean. In order to climb

Power, not speed, is the key to going up.

these freaky angles, you must drive the rear wheel into the ground rather than merely maintain traction with weight. Here's the deal.

1. Get in your lowest gear and approach the ascent at a walking pace. Don't think that speed is the answer. Traction is—this is why full-suspension bikes are often faster on climbs than hardtails, despite weighing more and sacrificing some pedal energy to suspension movement.

2. As you begin to angle upward, lean toward the stem as usual. But this time float your butt off the saddle. It should still touch, but not with any weight on it. Hover.

3. As the pitch increases, move your body forward until the nose of the saddle is the only part touching your butt. This extreme position guarantees that the front wheel will bite the ground instead of breaking loose and causing squirrelly steering. But it also means that the rear wheel has no weight pinning it to the turf. What to do?

4. With every downstroke of the pedals, pull the handlebar back (not up) into your chest—almost as if you are rowing the bike

like a boat, with the handlebar as an oar. This drives the rear wheel into the ground just as you apply power.

Synchronizing the handlebar pull with the pedal downstroke is the hardest part of the maneuver. It might seem impossible for a while. But once everything clicks, you'll stick to ascents like glue—in fact, the limit to what you can climb will be fitness rather than technique. Riding like this takes upper-body strength and the ability to either generate lots of power aerobically or to withstand many bursts of anaerobic effort (every time you pull the bar).

Back on Track

You're climbing great! Maybe you're finally going to clean this climb. Then you wobble into a rock, and suddenly you're dead in the middle of a steep pitch with one foot on the ground. Now what?

To get going again, you must first be in a low enough gear. If necessary, shift to a bigger cog (remember: In the back, a bigger cog is an easier gear) by clicking the shifter, lifting the rear of the bike with one hand on the saddle, and twirling the crankset with the clicked-in foot. (Be careful not to let the free pedal smack your calf.) It might help to lessen the slope by angling the bike across the trail.

On most trails, the side cut into the mountain is highest. Put the uphill foot on the ground so you won't fall down the slope if you lose balance. This position also means that you can sit on the saddle to get going, because the uphill leg has less distance to reach the ground. Place the downslope foot on the pedal, which should be rotated just past top dead center so you can apply a full power stroke to get going.

Next, look where you want to go. Pick something to aim at— maybe a rock or a trailside tree that's some distance ahead. Don't drop your head and stare 2 feet in front of your tire. Trust your peripheral vision to pick out the little details closer in.

Bend your elbows, relax your upper body, look ahead as you release the brakes and initiate the power stroke, and give the handlebar a little push to help the bike move forward. Immediately place your uphill foot on the pedal. Don't look down, and don't worry about clicking in. Just get some foot on the pedal and start pumping, applying power equally on both sides. If you fumble around trying to engage the cleat, you'll lose momentum and stall. You need some speed and stability so you can ease off pedal pressure momentarily. When you're pressing down hard, you can't slide your shoe into position.

24 >>>>

DOWNHILL THRILLS

For most developing riders, few mountain biking experiences are scarier than downhills. Think about it: The Earth's already unreliable stick-and-stone surface plunges away from you at a momentum-building angle that your brakes can't overcome. And even if you could stop halfway down, would you be able to safely put a foot down and keep from tumbling? Maybe. Maybe not. So you walk. You've dodged your fear—and a chance for unrivaled fun. Here are the steps you need to learn how to dance with the downhill demon.

Approach slowly. To gain confidence and experience, it's important that you control your descending speed. You can't do this if you're already exceeding your comfort zone as you drop in. On steep descents, the most your brakes can do is minimize acceleration, not slow you. Walking speed is a pace that often works. But don't approach so slowly that your front wheel stalls at the edge of the drop.

Set up. First, make sure that you're in a big enough gear to keep your chain from slapping against your bike or shaking loose. This is usually a middle chainring/largest cog or large chainring/middle cog combination. Next, set your crankarms horizontally so that a pedal doesn't become an impromptu anchor on a rock or log. Keep your elbows and knees relaxed and bent, letting your body's natural shock absorbers soak up jolts. Look past the rim and down the trail to a point you want to ride to. If you stare at a drop, a rut, or some other obstacle, you'll steer into it. That's how our eye–brain interface is wired.

Shift your weight back. As your bike begins angling down, slide toward the rear of the saddle. The steeper the descent, the more you should move back. On the sharpest dives, you might end up with your butt hanging above the rear wheel and the seat bumping your chest. Shift your weight to keep your center of gravity from pitching too far forward and upending you.

Adjust your weight shift. If you're like most newcomers, you'll move back farther than necessary the first few times you try this. If you go too far back, your front wheel becomes light and skittery and hard to control. Don't panic. Simply adjust your weight distribution by scooting forward. As you gain experience, you'll be able to fine-tune your control by subtle weight shifts—merely raising or lowering your chest, for instance.

Be an artful braker. Sudden movements are doom on descents. Strive for smoothness in all actions, including braking. It's best to begin with a controlled speed, but if you find yourself going too fast, don't panic and slam on the brakes—or you'll slam on the ground.

Use bent elbows and knees as natural shock absorbers.

You'll probably overuse the rear brake at first, locking the rear wheel and causing it to skid. This not only tears up the trail and wears the tire, it doesn't slow you and lessens your control. If the rear wheel skids, ease off and increase pressure on the front brake.

Most of your braking power comes from the front. As long as you have enough weight rearward, applying the front brake won't pitch you over the bar. If the front wheel starts to skid, ease off the lever until it begins rolling again, then tenderly resqueeze. If the skid continues, steer into it with subtle movements, just like you would in a car. Don't brake hard up front as you hit obstacles or roll over drops. The front wheel has more stability when it rolls freely.

Bounce back big. When you fall—and you will—walk to a more level spot where you can get back on. Point your bike across the trail, squeeze the brakes as you climb aboard, and turn downhill. Don't make more than three or four steep runs each session. You'll start making mistakes just because you're tired.

Roll out and regroup. As you reach the bottom of a downhill, begin returning to a neutral position over the saddle (if you don't, you'll have too much weight rearward) and let go of your brakes. If you're smooth and fearless, you can milk much momentum from the runout of even a moderate descent. Fun, huh?

Five No-No's

Here are the things you want to avoid when descending.

1. Don't try to steer by turning the handlebar. If you do, the bike gets all unstable and uppity. Try controlling your direction by shifting your weight sideways. Expert riders steer their bikes simply by moving their hips. Give it a shot. You initially might have to overcompensate with big weight shifts to get a feel for it.

2. Don't brake at the wrong time. Squeezing the brakes right before or after a big drop-off or before a big rock or log is a panic move— pure instinct. You'll probably get away with it if you're in the funky, learning, way-low position. But notice how it punches your bike to a stop and makes you jerky. Condition yourself to ignore instinct.

3. Don't worry too much about your line. Gravity is going to pull your bike down the hill no matter how stinky your route. There's a tendency to bail as soon as you lose the best line—the cleanest, smoothest, most apparent path. When you get all jacked around, hang in there and see what happens. Let the bike roll. If you see an opening to slip back into the good line, take it—but pay more attention to the line you're already in.

4. Don't get stiff. This is another instinct you have to train out of yourself. When you're tight, the bike transmits its shocks into your body, which transmits them back, and things are a mess. Instead of absorbing a bump, you let it steer the bike for you. Bad idea. You need to be the pilot. It's hard to diagnose tightness by thinking about your elbows and knees. If the bike suddenly seems out of control—hammering you with hard vertical blows—and your vision gets jumpy, try loosening your joints. If that doesn't work, you're probably going too fast for your skill level. Slow down a little.

5. Don't bail when you get sideways. Your bike is going to throw all kinds of new tricks at you on descents. One of the coolest and most exhilarating is the first time it starts taking you down the trail sideways. Don't bail. Loosen the brakes, shift your weight to the high side and slightly toward the center of the trail, and you can make it.

25

PART THE WATERS

Riding your bike through a stream can be a refreshing splash on a hot day or a treacherous dunking that leaves you soaked as your bike floats down the torrent. Knowing when to ride and when to wade requires the stream-reading ability of a fly fisherman (and some common sense, too). Here's how to avoid total submersion.

Scout it out. Most stream crossings are located at the bottom of a hill, so you'll probably approach fast. Slow down and determine where you'll enter and where you'll exit. Come to a complete stop, if necessary. You can always back up and try it again after you have spied the line. Let your bike-handling skills and environmental factors (don't trash a delicate bank) be your guides.

Here are some things to think about before going in.

Are the rocks so big that your front wheel could get trapped? Could you smash into a submerged boulder (a surefire recipe for a damaged rear derailleur)?

Can you not see the bottom because the water is too discolored or deep? If you can't, test the depth with a stick before venturing in.

Is the water so swift that it could sweep the wheels out from under you?

Is the stream bottom so muddy that you'll cause permanent ruts?

If wading is the right choice, carry your bike high enough so that it stays completely dry. It should be on the downstream side so that if you slip (usually in the downstream direction), it won't land on top of you. In deep water, hold the entire bike above your head.

Find a line. If your choice is to ride through, avoid the direct line as often as you can. Why? Crossings that see frequent traffic, especially those shared with recreational off-road vehicles, will often have a pool that's been dug out right in the middle, with a treacherously soft bottom waiting to grab your wheels and toss you into the drink.

Instead, look slightly up- or downstream for shallower or rockier surfaces. A good bet is the shallow riffle that's usually below the pool. You can see all the rocks and maneuver around them.

Watch the bottom. Check out the bottom of the stream, too. You'll encounter everything from mud and sand to boulders and roots—and they're all slicker than ice. Pebbles and small cobbles are easier to ride across (if they're not covered with slimy algae). When the rocks get bigger, picking a good line is harder. You might be able to weave through a rock garden on land, but it's considerably harder when the boulders are wet. In general, your knowledge of the area will help you discriminate.

Make the crossing. Once you have determined the best line, build some momentum, shift to a gear that will enable you to accelerate in midstream if necessary, release the brakes, and go for it. Your goal is to get across by pedaling as little as possible and preferably not at all. Get into a low, crouched position, out of the saddle, with your elbows and knees bent. Imitate a cat ready to pounce. Be light on the front wheel, with your weight slightly to the rear, as if you're descending. Make sure the crankarms are parallel to the water to keep your feet relatively dry and to give you the best chance of clearing rocks.

After the bath. Remember that once you've forded a stream, you still carry some of the stream with you. Mud or sand can make your tires slippery, so don't expect to arrive on the other side with the same traction you had going in.

Ease into your dry-land pedaling—don't give a big power stroke as soon as you reach solid ground. It could be several minutes before your tires and rims dry out, so be conservative while braking and ma-

Momentum is the key to successful stream crossing.

neuvering until you know that your rig is back to normal.

Two more points: First, before a ride that has several stream crossings, make sure that your pedals are well lubed. Clipless pedals work best when the springs are covered with grease. Sure, sand and dirt will stick to them so that they look like lollipops dropped in a sandbox, but they're a lot safer. A dry pedal is a dangerous and unpredictable pedal. You don't want to get to the other side, grinning about your achievement, only to fall over because you can't release in a pinch.

Second, avoid riding in water that is deep enough to submerge the crankset. The movement caused by pedaling will let water through the bearing seals and degrade the grease inside the bottom bracket. Your hub bearings and chain lube will be history, too.

26

CRASH AND LEARN

Advice on how to crash is usually worthless—dripping with obvious tips such as "Know your limits," and "Be careful on unfamiliar trails." If you can't figure that stuff out for yourself, you're probably too dumb to pedal anyway. What would be helpful is some real advice: the best ways to try to land, some tips for bailing out and maybe stopping safely, and how to entertain yourself while you're soaring through the air.

Fall like a tree trunk. Think of what happens to a tree when it falls. Branches snap, but the trunk is just fine. A rider's instinct is to brace against an impact, to reach out toward the onrushing ground. That's bad. Arms separate from shoulders or break apart. Fingers dangle. Hands flop. It sounds painful, and it is.

A lot of crash experts recommend curling into a ball—pulling in your arms and legs and head like one of those "rolly" pill bugs you find under wet logs—but this may not always be possible. If not, at least have the presence of mind not to extend your limbs. You'll still land hard, probably harder than if you could become a compact ball of flesh, but you'll land on the solid parts instead of the spindly ones.

Roll when you land. After you hit, roll with the momentum unless you're really close to a cliff, a highway, or a hibernating bear. This helps dissipate the impact. The alternative is skidding, which creates lots of friction between your soft body and many harder things. Your body loses—mostly skin. Also, you're more likely to snag body parts on an obstruction. That's how you dislocate stuff. Although rolling makes you travel farther, you're moving lighter over the ground. Of course, if you're plunging down a slope, you should try to skid and catch yourself on something.

Stay with your bike, sometimes. On a garden-variety endo or any other idiocy that shoots you forward, consider holding onto the handlebar and not clicking out of the pedals. You and the bike will stay together and twirl in a choreographed pretzel of safety and low impact. You don't always want to do this, and it's hard to tell you when

Try to land on your solid parts, not your spindly ones.

not to, except to say that after you try it once or twice, you'll get a feel for when it will work. But you have to commit to it. When you do it halfway—like clicking out but hanging onto the bar—the bike can get tangled with you pretty good. This only causes more damage.

Big-ring the descents. Using the big ring on the descents stops chain slap, but it also covers those sharp teeth on the outer chainring. Would you rather scrape your leg across a greasy chain or a buzz saw?

Bail and forget your bike. If you lose control on a downhill or a flat stretch at cruising speed, you can simply slip off the back of your bike and let it roll away. If you hit the ground with your feet moving you can run yourself to a stop. This is a cool move, except you'll look like one of the Keystone Kops and your friends will laugh at you for the rest of the ride. But it works. Similarly, when your bike stops short from ramming something, you can vault the handlebar and run out your momentum. But that's much tougher. If you don't clear the bar with both feet, you'll splat your face on the ground like a water balloon.

Avoid falling directly sideways. Try to disperse some of the force of a fall by landing slightly forward or backward instead of sideways. If you fall to the side, you're more likely to land on the tip of your collarbone—a piece of calcium not really built to withstand that kind of impact.

Just stop. Once a crash sequence begins, things get worse for quite a while before they get better. The sooner you interrupt the process, the better. For example, you would be wise to stop at the top of an impossible descent, fall over, and scrape your hand rather than dive over the edge, lose control, and rip off an ear. This is tough advice, because you also avoid a lot of crashes by riding through them—getting away with stuff that you thought would mutilate you. And, ultimately, if you generally try to ride out your mistakes, you'll be a better rider for it. You'll merely be a safer rider if you don't.

27 >>>

PACE YOURSELF LIKE A PRO

Pacing is one of the most important things to remember in a mountain bike race or any lengthy off-road ride—and it was crucial in helping Colorado's **Susan DeMattei** win a bronze medal at the Atlanta Olympics in 1996. Here's what she says about how to conserve energy and ride strong to the finish.

"I tried to treat the Olympic cross-country race like any other, and not get overly hyped. But right away, things began going wrong—I started at the back of the pack, and I couldn't get my foot in the pedal. I'm not typically good at superfast starts, anyway, so all of a sudden I found myself almost last. But at that point I told myself, 'Hey, you have 2 hours to go—don't be stupid.' I just tried to save myself and pass people at opportune moments. Then Paola Pezzo (the eventual winner) started to ride away from us. I tried to go after her for a few seconds, but felt myself slipping into oxygen debt. I had to pull in the reins and go at a speed that felt more appropriate. That was the right thing to do, because it enabled me to last until the end and win the bronze."

This kind of self-knowledge doesn't apply just to racing. Even on a recreational ride, it's tempting to throw caution to the wind—particularly if you're feeling good. You tend to get hyped and go as hard as possible right from the start. Who doesn't? But more often than not, you'll regret it later. You have to stay within your means.

Just remember the old saying: It doesn't matter where you are in the first half of a ride or race but where you are in the second half. Here are some pointers that will make you happy in the home stretch.

Get in gear. Before the Olympics, I had an opportunity to preview the Atlanta mountain bike course and use the German-made SRM PowerMeter power-measuring crankset. It was the first time the device had been used for mountain biking, and the results were fascinating. The US Olympic Committee's sports scientists downloaded all the data and discovered that the biggest energy robbers are short, steep climbs—especially if you're not a rider who uses a fast cadence. This really opened my eyes to the unique physiological demands of mountain biking. You need to be smart about gear selection. Don't hammer over hills in a big gear, because that will sap you. I prefer to settle into a gear that feels almost too easy, so I still have something left at the end. I have no reservations about going to the granny chainring, but for some people it's a matter of pride to stay in the middle ring. All of a sudden, however, they'll be pedaling at a cadence of 40 rpm.

It's a myth that standing in a big gear is faster than sitting and spinning. I like to keep a steady cadence of about 80 rpm, no matter what the steepness of the climb. The only time to push a slightly bigger gear in the middle ring is for a short roller, where you can stand, crest the rise with a few strong strokes, and keep your momentum going down the other side.

Keep pedaling on descents. When you get to a long descent, the tendency is to think, "Great, here's where I can rest my legs and recover." But if you keep pedaling lightly, you'll gain lots of time and still recover. Shift to a big gear and let it roll. If it's a race, and you can gain 15 seconds per lap by pedaling lightly, that will really add up. And you won't kill yourself in the process.

Avoid the lemming syndrome. Don't become obsessed with staying on someone else's wheel—particularly in the first part of a ride or race. You have to learn what your limits and abilities are. Many times, if you let that person go and maintain your own pace, you'll see him again later on. Remember the tortoise and the hare.

Let it flow. To save energy, it's important to be conscious of what your upper body is doing. I've even had my form videotaped to ensure that I stay relaxed. During a race or ride, you should periodically go through a relaxation drill: Take a deep breath, let your shoulders drop, and release the tension through your arms and hands. Don't use a death grip. Never fight your bike—instead, let it flow beneath you.

Stay fueled and hydrated. One of the keys to going the distance is to eat and drink enough. This enables your muscles to work better.

I always have a good breakfast before a race or long ride, and sometimes I'll snack close to the start.

Then, drink throughout the event. I have two bottle cages on my bike. In a race, I carry one bottle of water and have someone hand me another bottle partway through that contains defizzed Coke, because that's palatable to me. Also, after a hard ride or race, I like to have a carbohydrate drink to immediately restore glycogen to my muscles.

Train for stamina. Here's a favorite workout that helps ensure that I can go the distance: I ride for 90 minutes at what I call a medium-hard pace. Let's say that my race pace, or anaerobic threshold, is about 155 beats per minute. These medium-hard rides would be done at about 145 bpm. If you don't have a heart-rate monitor, shoot for something below race pace—not flat out, but fast enough that you have to struggle a bit. The minute your mind wanders and you're not thinking about the pace, you're probably not going hard enough.

These rides make me more tired than doing intervals. They're pretty depleting, so you should be sure to stay well fueled and well hydrated. Do this workout no more than twice a week; once a week is enough to see benefits. Start with 20 to 30 minutes if you're new to cycling, and work up from there.

A powerful but relaxed effort propelled DeMattei to an Olympic medal.

Find your perfect edge. When you truly know yourself, you'll be able to ride on the perfect edge at the end of a ride. There's an old saying that if you're able to sprint at the end, then you didn't go hard enough. That's how it usually is for me. I just don't have it in me to go any harder in the final few minutes, and I figure that's just about right.

28

MIDSEASON REVIVAL

You began the season with great intentions and infinite gusto. But now you're nowhere near your goal and are ready to say screw it. Somehow, your ambition began to slip away. First you missed a ride. Then another. Then Jerry Springer switched time slots and Burger King ran that 89-cent special and now summer is here and you're nowhere near your goal and it's probably too late to start over.

Hang on. Maybe you've blown some valuable riding time, but it's not too late to regroup. Experts say that you can see significant improvement in your fitness after 1 to 3 months of regular training (depending on your goals and starting point). This means you could be satisfyingly operational by midsummer. You might even be able to salvage that banner year, although your performance won't peak until much later—maybe even in the fall.

Check the descriptions to find the level that comes closest to your ambition. Then you'll discover the key concept that will become your season saver. And you'll get advice from New England's **Paul Curley**, a former road and mountain bike pro turned coach. In fact, Curley has created a special "ultimate workout" that can be calibrated to any fitness level. He gives you a stock training schedule with all the information you need to customize it.

Level 1: Just Diving In

You just want to ride. You bought a new bike, met a cool person who's into cycling, or finally became sufficiently humiliated by your flab. This is supposed to be the start of something new, but you just can't get out on the trail enough—and every time you do, parts of your body ache so much you regret it.

You don't really need a training schedule yet. You need time on the bike—something you probably know but aren't approaching correctly.

You're overestimating how much time you need and not riding until you can devote an hour or more, which limits you to weekends and infrequent weekdays. The key is logging consistent saddle time, and it doesn't have to be much. You can begin building endurance and acclimating your body to the bike with rides as short as 15 minutes.

Try riding just 15 minutes each day the first week of your comeback. The next week, you can cut back to 4 or 5 days but increase each session to 20 to 30 minutes, if possible. You can even break the time into two 15-minute sessions (morning and evening, for instance). Experts generally suggest exercising for at least 20 consecutive minutes, but at this level, splitting the effort won't matter. What's most important is the combined saddle time that will condition your butt, hands, back, neck, shoulders, and legs to riding.

It will also build the base of endurance you'll need when you're ready for actual training (which should be in 4 to 8 weeks). For now, do your rides at an aerobic level—60 to 85 percent of your heart's maximum rate. You don't need a heart-rate monitor to measure this, or even a watch to take your pulse. Work hard enough that your heart rate increases, but not so hard that you can't talk. It's okay if you want to intersperse harder efforts, but it's not mandatory.

Level 2: Going Deeper

You signed up for a mountain-biking adventure vacation and don't want to embarrass yourself (not to mention paying big bucks to spend the whole trip in physical misery). Or you want to whip your friends' butts or finally shed those last few extra pounds and get in the kind of shape you've always told yourself you would.

Realize that you need training just as much as a racer, and commit to riding that way three to five times per week.

You don't need to be as intense or focused as a racer, but you need to be as committed. Your fitness plateaus at a weak point if you ride around only when you feel like it, or even if you make an effort to ride regularly 4 to 6 days per week but without at least a rough plan to strengthen different parts of your system.

"It's important for people to start some kind of complete program right away—if they check out okay medically," says Curley. "The intensity of a trained racer might not be there, but even someone in poor condition is capable of doing a max-effort sprint for 15 to 20 seconds and seeing big benefits from it. Once you're used to riding a bike, I don't think you need to waste time riding 1,000 easy miles to build a base before trying intervals or sprinting, as some coaches advise."

Incorporate Curley's full program of power, speed, endurance, and recovery, scaling the intensities and length to fit your condition. Also, "Group rides are mandatory. At least once a week, go out with a group that includes people better than you. Other riders show you things and push you further than you can push yourself," says Curley.

Level 3: Making a Splash

You want to do a race and finish in the top half, gain status in the "A" group of local recreational riders, or leave that group behind and join the serious racing crowd.

"This is the point where you need to start thinking about your pulse," says Curley. "You really need a heart-rate monitor. And— here's the key—you must use it to dictate the pace of your effort instead of just watching it while you do whatever effort you want.

"A lot of riders I coach have never correlated their monitors to a training method. They're using it for curiosity or distraction— watching the meter perform instead of making their bodies perform at a certain pulse rate. Big difference. You need to know on any given day of the week what pulse rate you should be riding at. At times, it will be uncomfortable, but ultimately, it's more rewarding."

Level 4: Finding Buried Treasure

You want to win a local race, place well in a national event, or become one of the best riders in your region.

"Road," states Curley, with the monosyllabic command of great coaches. "No way around it. Someone who rides only a mountain bike is limited to a sub-max fitness level. Mountain biking beats up your body too much to let you get the kind of ongoing, sustained cardiovascular workouts you need. The environment is less controllable, too, so it's harder to hit a prescribed heart rate when you need to. Plus, if you're spending 15 hours a week training on your mountain bike, your risk of injury goes up.

"The mountain bikers I've coached who are competitive at the world level might do a whole week of training, all on the road, but I wouldn't advocate that for the amateur level. If you're going to race every weekend, maybe your Wednesday ride, which is the most intense of the week, can be a structured off-road ride."

The Ultimate 15-Minute Workout

You don't have time for a training schedule, but still want one lung-busting, fitness-improving workout? Here it is, in Curley's own words because he knows exactly what he's talking about.

"Find a local trail you can complete in 10 to 15 minutes in time-trial mode. This is race pace or a little above. Or, mark off part of a larger trail.

"Go out with a bunch of riders of all abilities. The slowest one starts first, then the second slowest, all the way up. Do this after a warmup of 10 to 20 minutes. Afterward, the stronger riders can train more if they want. This kind of motivational pursuit while everyone is fresh keeps everyone in the game, but it also hammers everyone, no matter how fit they are.

"The higher your level of fitness, the more reps you might do. It's almost impossible for someone to go out alone and go as hard as they can for an hour. But if you have a little loop and a group of committed riders that can do it in 10 minutes, you might do six heats."

Weekly Training Schedule

This is a guide, not a legal order. Make it fit your life (not the other way around).

Monday: Rest or active recovery

Tuesday: Sprints

Wednesday: Intervals

Thursday: Steady riding (endurance)

Friday: Rest or active recovery

Saturday: Sprints/intervals (focus on intensity)

Sunday: Intervals/steady (focus on endurance)

Sprints. These can be done for power or speed. Power is the explosive burst that lets you rocket up that short, steep hill or fly off a start line. Speed is the ability to go fast without becoming inefficient.

Sample Power Sprint: Do hill repeats. Pick a section of trail with a steep hill not longer than 25 seconds at max effort. Your cadence shouldn't exceed 80 rpm. The first week, do 6 to 10 repeats (recovering for 60 seconds between each repeat). The next week, do 1 or 2 more repeats.

Sample Speed Sprint: Find a flat road or short piece of singletrack that you can ride at your max in excess of 100 rpm. Do 6 to 10 repeats. Recover for 60 seconds. If your pedal stroke stays together at a cadence this high, your normal cadence will become much more efficient.

Intervals. These are also hard efforts—slightly easier than sprints but sustained longer. By holding yourself within plus or minus five beats of your anaerobic threshold—about 85 to 90 percent of your maximum heart rate—you improve your ability to ride at race pace. For instance, if you train yourself to ride for 10 minutes at 180 bpm, there's a good chance you can do an hour at 170 bpm.

Sample Interval: Six minutes of hard riding on your favorite technical trail followed by 4 minutes of recovery, repeated 2 to 10 times (based on your fitness). The recovery interval is key. If you don't let lactic acid drain from your muscles, you won't be able to ride as hard for as long.

By doing an interval on a trail, you also train your technical skill at high speeds, so that when you slow down to race pace, you can concentrate on propelling your bike, while control becomes automatic.

Endurance. This is a long, steady effort at an aerobic level (60 to 85 percent of your max heart rate). It helps your body recover from intense efforts, increases your ability to ride aerobically, and trains your body to burn fat as a fuel. "This is very helpful early in a rider's career," says Curley. "Your body has to be taught to burn fat when it's depleted of glycogen."

Rest or active recovery. Rest is inactivity. Active recovery is a brisk walk, a short spin, or anything that exercises your body without stressing it. Active recovery is generally better for sore muscles.

Workload. Curley recommends training in cycles of 3 to 5 weeks. Add about 10 percent more riding time each week during this period, then take a rest week where you do only 40 to 50 percent of what you did the previous week.

Begin a new cycle at about the workload just below that of week two in the previous cycle. For example: The workload of week seven is just under the workload of week two. "This is a cycle that's been proven throughout the world," Curley says. "It's been shown to work in labs and in races."

Less fit riders might need their rest period after week three. The intensities shouldn't vary, though duration will. An aerobic workout should always be at 60 to 85 percent of your maximum heart rate, a sprint should always be at max effort, and so on. The fitter you become, the more time you dedicate—and that's a number only you can pick for your lifestyle.

DUAL SCHOOL

What's your mental picture of riding a dual-suspension bike? It probably includes big air, screaming downhills, and launching over wheel-swallowing erosion ditches. But it's a misconception to think that dual suspension is useful only in such extreme terrain. The truth is that dual suspension works for all types of riding, especially given the recent advances in shock technology. Here are the keys to getting the most out of a dual-suspension bike, no matter what type of rider you are.

Sit down and let the bike do the work. Especially on climbs, dual suspension is most effective when you stay seated and let it absorb rough terrain. Climbing in the saddle is more efficient because you aren't supporting your body weight—all of your energy goes into heading uphill. Dualies make seated climbing more comfortable, too, because the rear wheel follows the contours of the terrain and the saddle doesn't bash your crotch.

Pedal in circles, not squares. Some riders just stomp on the pedals, letting their body weight push the crankarms around. But if you practice turning full, smooth circles, you'll eliminate most of the energy-sapping bounce associated with dual suspension. Check Chapter 6 for tips on how to pedal more smoothly.

Save your energy. Dual suspension really comes into its own on climbs with little ledges, logs, or roots that interrupt the trail's smoothness. On a hardtail, you have to pull up on the front end, then shift your weight forward to get the rear wheel over these obstacles. These movements use extra energy—both physical and mental. Instead, stay seated on a dualie and simply ride up and over the ledge. Even if you must stand, try to avoid elevating the front wheel or shifting your weight.

Save energy by riding over the small stuff.

Adjust the suspension. You generally pay a premium for dual suspension, so why not get all the travel possible? Proper tuning is the key to maximum riding performance. The shocks should be adjusted so you're using all the travel only on the biggest hits. You don't want to bottom out very often—but then again, if you never bottom out, you aren't benefiting from the suspension's full range.

In general, the shocks on a new dualie are set up for a 160- to 190-pound rider. Adjusting preload (spring pressure) will help tailor the ride to a different weight. But for a real featherweight or a Clydesdale, the stock adjustments may need to be tweaked. See Suspension Setup, opposite page, for more tips on adjusting suspension.

Ratchet the pedals. Dual suspension will tempt you to pedal through anything, so be careful not to catch a pedal on a rock or the high side of a trail. Some of the sport's nastiest crashes have been from bashing a pedal: The bike jumps to one side and down you go. Learn to ratchet the pedals, which means to take a partial stroke, backpedal, and take another partial stroke. The pedals never travel all the way down to the bottom of the stroke, which makes it easier to get through a tricky section. Or, if you have enough momentum, you can simply coast.

Go wide in the turns. A dualie's generous suspension travel means that you can push the bike down with the outside pedal and carve turns like a skier. But watch out—long-travel forks make the head-tube angle steepen when the fork is compressed, quickening the steering response. If you brake hard on a steep switchback, the fork will dive and the turning radius will suddenly be too tight. Compensate for heavy front brake use by taking a wider line around the corner.

Beware the "yee-hah!" factor. Dual suspension lets you go fast in most terrains even if you don't have great technique. That's fine, as long as you realize that if you do fall, you'll be really flying and it will hurt a lot more. Don't get in over your head.

Suspension Setup

No matter how much you adapt your technique to dual suspension, it's not going to help unless your suspension is properly tuned to your weight, riding style, and terrain. In the early days of suspension, tuning was best tackled by specialized gurus. But the advent of easily adjustable air shocks has made suspension tuning no more complicated than inflating a tire. Still, there are some basic ground rules every rider should adhere to, and **Chris "Monkey" Vasquez**, who's been tuning suspension for some of the world's best downhill and cross-country racers for over a dozen years, knows exactly what they are.

Buy the right bike. Sounds painfully obvious, but Monkey says that many riders simply get the wrong bike for their riding style. "You need to consider what type of riding you want to do now, and what type you're going to want to do down the road," says Monkey. "And don't be cheap. If you want a Ferrari, don't buy a Nissan."

Set your sag. Sag is the amount of shock movement that occurs when you sit on the bike. Monkey recommends attaching a zip-tie to the body of the rear shock and one of the fork stanchions (the shiny, inside part of the fork). For freeriding and downhilling, you want the shocks to sag about 30 percent of their total travel. For cross-country racing, look for about 10 percent sag. And for general riding, 15 percent to 20 percent is a good starting point.

Know the controls. If you can afford it, Monkey suggests buying a bike equipped with shocks that boast multiple adjustments, such as compression and rebound damping, which help control how the bike responds to bump forces. "Make sure your shop shows you how to adjust the shocks," says Monkey. "And these days, all the shock manufacturers have tuning info on their Web sites. Use it."

Experiment. "The biggest mistake most riders make is getting on their bikes and riding without adjusting suspension," says Monkey. "Don't be afraid to touch it; close down the compression damping and ride around to see what that feels like. Then, open it up all the way and ride with it like that. Play with your rebound damping, too. Small adjustments can make a huge difference."

Know how to compensate. "If your hands are hurting, decrease compression damping so your fork will be more active," explains Monkey. "If it feels like your fork is trying to buck you off, increase your rebound damping, so it returns to the top of the suspension stroke more slowly. The more you play around with your suspension, the better you'll understand how to tune it to specific terrain, and the better your bike will ride."

Don't wait. "A lot of people are afraid to jump in, because they think suspension is going to get better and better and they want to wait for the next big thing," says Monkey. "Thing is, suspension is really, really dialed right now. It might get lighter, and it might get more expensive, but it's honestly hard to imagine it getting much better in terms of performance. If you want it, go for it."

WANNA RACE?

One of the reasons mountain biking is great is that there aren't many absolutes. There's no way to tell you that to dig the sport you must ride a dual-suspension bike (or even a hardtail) or lay tracks at Moab or learn to bunny-hop. It's your groove, baby.

But racing is an absolute. Every mountain biker should race at least once.

Why? Because racing makes you faster, fitter, and more skilled. It hones you quicker than anything else can—faster even than reading books or magazines, watching videos, riding with those great friends who always have advice, or discovering helpful stuff on your own by dumb luck. Racing also initiates you into a part of the mountain-biking family you might be missing. Show up on a start line on a rigid bike, wearing a T-shirt and running shoes, and you still get to ride the same singletrack as the best riders in the race. And those riders will talk to you before and after—sometimes even during—the race. Why? Because you're one of them.

But those are rationalizations for continual racing. Even if you think you'll never do another race, you should enter at least one. Because racing is a mix of everything that's exalted and hideous about mountain biking, you need to taste it once.

There's intense pain and joy separated by mere pedal strokes. There's passion. Tragedy. Comedy. Speed. Spectacular crashes you laugh off. Adrenaline. A moment when you dig deeper into yourself than you knew you could and pull out something solid that keeps you going, and another moment when you dig just as deep and find nothing. The start will be unlike anything you've ever felt on a mountain bike. The finish will be like everything you've ever felt on a mountain bike.

Here's what you need to know to get in.

- To find a race, look in regional bike magazines or newsletters, or stop by a bike shop. You might not think there are any nearby events, but you'll be surprised. In fact, the National Off-Road Bicycle Association (NORBA) sanctions more than 1,000 races each season. In addition, local clubs may have weekly low-key training races.

- Races usually cost $15 to $50 to enter. You don't get much for the money—sometimes a T-shirt or water bottle. The prizes are usually bike parts or clothing and sometimes go as deep as 15th place. But don't be surprised if only the top three to five finishers get stuff.

- You don't need a racing license. A yearly license from NORBA costs $65. But for just one event, you can get a special "1-day license" that tacks about 10 bucks onto your entry fee.

- Race Sport class. The lower-level Beginner races are short— usually 4 to 10 miles—and less intimidating. But Sport races are more fun. The courses are more challenging and more varied, so you get more experience for your entry fee. There are also more riders—the Sport class is more crowded than any other. If you get into racing and like it enough to go for wins, you can always drop back into the Beginner class where you'll be more competitive.

Race Day

Okay, you're in. Now you're on your own. So much of the race will be beyond your control that it's impossible to give you a strategy or race plan. But you can do better and avoid some common mistakes by following these tips.

Register early. If you wait until attendance peaks, you spend big hunks of your prerace time standing in line.

Scout the course. The pros do at least one full lap so they know how long the climbs are, where the technical sections are, where the best places to pass are, and so on. But if you don't have the time or ambition, just ride 15 minutes from the start, then turn around and ride 15 minutes from the finish. At least you'll know that much. If the course map highlights really tough sections, sometimes you can cut across the course (instead of following it) to get a look at them. But then you're so close to preriding the whole thing anyway that you might as well go ahead and ride it all.

Warm up. When you plant yourself under the start banner, your bright new jersey should be wet with sweat, your legs should be loose, and your heart should be primed so it doesn't have to jump from 60 to 190 bpm. You can accomplish all of this with a 20- to 60-minute warmup of moderate effort with two or three hard bursts.

Fill a spare tube halfway with air. Fold it four times and stuff it in your jersey pocket. This saves minutes if you flat during the race.

Fill your water bottle or hydration backpack. Use a half-and-half mixture of energy drink or fruit juice and water. Sometimes the feed stations have energy drinks; sometimes they just have water. By the way: No way do you have the time or luxury to eat anything solid during the race.

Line up. If you want to get a place at the front, you usually need to poke your way in at least 25 minutes ahead of the start time. Which means you stand around undoing all the good of your warmup. That's all right if you do okay starting cold. If not, you'll have to arrive later and settle for a midpack position.

Choose your enemies. Look around and pick out some riders who appear to be about as fit as you are, ride a similar bike, and wear about the same type of equipment. These are your opponents. Chase them and you will go faster.

Control your amps. Many first-timers feel the race adrenaline and ride like pros for 150 yards, then explode into itty-bitty pieces. You need to start fast, because everyone wants to get to the singletrack section near the front, but don't go at a pace that's beyond your experience. Ride like you ride.

Control your ascents. Don't blow up on the first hill. Mountain bike races are like road time trials in that to do your best, you have to apportion your energy. Hills are where you can use up way too much, especially early in the race, when you're still feeling frisky.

Control your descents. Downhills are great places to make up time on those skinny climbers who are kicking your butt. Unfortunately, descents are also carnage central for this same reason. Once again: Ride like you ride.

Pass politely. Don't pass when there's no room to pass. You might wreck or wreck someone else.

With thousands of races nationwide, there's bound to be one that's near you.

Even if you don't, you look like an overfocused idiot. Let other people pass without impedance if they say, "Track," or "On your left," or "Excuse me, I was wondering if I might blow by you." If you block, you're a jackass.

Take clean clothes. After the race, you will lie on the grass regaining the use of your brain, retalking the highlights with the people who finished near you, and staring in undisguised admiration at your muddy, dusty, bloody, quivering legs. That's acceptable for a while, but soon you should wipe down and change into fresh clothes because only posers display filthy racewear all day. Go get your carbo replenishment drink so your muscles recover better. And maybe, just maybe, start thinking about another race.

THE PRO SPEAKS

As the top US finisher in the 2004 Olympic mountain bike cross-country race, it's safe to say that **Todd Wells** knows a thing or two about going fast on a bike. The GT/Hyundai-sponsored rider hails from Durango, where he hones his fitness on some of the sweetest trails in the free world.

Wells may have it easy now, living the good life of a sponsored racer, but it wasn't always so. A few years ago, he was working a full time-plus job at IBM and squeezing his training into the short hours before and after work. Sound familiar? With that experience under his helmet, we figured Wells would be a good pick to share his favorite workouts for time-strapped racers.

The Endurance Ride

Wells works on his endurance primarily in the off season. "Once racing starts, I use the races themselves as endurance workouts," says Wells. "If I take a break from racing in the summer, I try to touch base with my endurance foundation with some long rides."

For Wells, an endurance ride might last as long as 5 hours; for you, it need only be twice as long as the longest event you're targeting. In other words, if your longest race is projected to take an hour to complete, shoot for an endurance threshold of 2 hours.

To do this, slowly increase the duration of your longest ride, adding no more than 15 percent each week. And keep the intensity low: "My endurance rides are all at about 65 percent to 70 percent of my maximum. If I go harder than that, I risk overtraining," explains Wells. And if the champ risks it, so do you.

The Group Ride

With his endurance base built, Wells begins to join the group rides that troll the mountain roads and trails around Durango. What's so great about group rides? "Group rides offer a tremendous variety of pace. You're going slow, then you're going fast, then you're going faster, then slow," says Wells. "And the added stimulation of other riders makes it easier to dig deep. It's like doing intervals, without having to go out there and ride up the same hill 10 times. Look, intervals pretty much suck—when's the last time you heard someone come home from intervals talking about what a great ride they had? That happens all the time on group rides, and the quality of the workout is the same or higher." One caveat: "There's not really any such thing as an 'easy' group ride," says Wells. "You've got to be careful not to do them too often—one a week is plenty—or you'll cook yourself."

The Recovery Ride

Believe it or not, the humble recovery ride is probably the most important workout in Wells's arsenal. "When I'm racing every weekend, almost every ride I do is a recovery ride. It takes a lot longer to recover from racing than people realize." What's a recovery ride? For Wells, it might be an hour and a half, twice a day, at less than 70 percent of his max. For you, it's more likely to be an hour at less than 70 percent. And yes, one recovery ride a day will do.

The Commute

Wells's secret weapon when he worked at IBM was his commute. "I'd head out early and tack on an extra loop to hit the distance I needed for the day," he recalls. "When you're working, you've gotta squeeze everything you can out of the day. People equate commuting with easy riding, but you can do real training on a commute. Think about all the time you waste sitting in your car. Turn that into training time and you're guaranteed to get better."

MOUNTAIN BIKING POSITION

Roadies are known for refining their position down to the millimeter. Mountain bikers tend to approach things more casually. There's nothing wrong with that, but it's still a good idea to examine your position carefully, then stick to the numbers. The main exception is if you are a young rider who occasionally needs to adjust for a growing body. Otherwise, most of us can set our position and forget it—unless there is a good reason to experiment (such as an injury or change in equipment). If you decide to make a modification, do it in small increments and test the new position in all kinds of terrains and situations. Get one thing right before moving to the next. If you make multiple changes all at once, you won't be sure what's working and what isn't.

There are riders who make themselves crazy trying to find the "perfect" position. It probably doesn't exist. A change in handlebar height, for example, can feel a little awkward at first. Don't worry about it, just get used to it once you're confident that you're within the standard guidelines. Realize that you won't feel perfect all the time on every ride, so resist the temptation to constantly tinker. Be certain of specific needs before you make a change.

1. **Frame size.** In case of spontaneous (and potentially painful) dismounts, there should be at least 2 inches of clearance between your crotch and the top tube. To measure, wear your cycling shoes and stand with the bike between your legs. Bikes with sloping top tubes may create even more clearance. For these, make sure that you can raise the saddle to the correct height without exceeding the maximum-extension line on the seatpost. You must also be able to achieve the proper reach (see step 7).

2. Saddle height. You'll need these props: a calculator, pencil, book, and metric tape measure. It also helps to have an assistant, so invite a friend over with his bike and you can both nail your positions. First, measure your inseam this way: Stand with bare feet about 6 inches apart and your back against a wall. Place the book between your legs with one edge flat to the wall, then slide it up until it's snug in your crotch. Mark the wall at the top corner of the book. Measure from the floor to the mark (your inseam length), then multiply this number by 0.883. The result is the proper distance from the center of the crankarm axle to the top of the saddle, measured in line with the seatpost. Remember, this is a universal concept of "proper," so don't be afraid to listen to your body and deviate from the norm.

3. Fore/aft saddle position. First, a rule: Don't move the seat backward or forward to compensate for improper reach (the combined length of the top tube and stem). Instead, the fore/aft adjustment is for establishing your position relative to the pedals. Put your bike on an indoor trainer or next to a wall. Climb on, wearing your cycling shoes. Sit normally in the center of the saddle. Clip into the pedals and position the crankarms horizontally. Have your friend drop a string with something small but heavy on the end from the front of your forward leg's kneecap. The string should touch the end of the crankarm. This is the neutral, or 0, position, which works well for most riders. If you like to push bigger gears with a slower cadence, a knee position up to 6 cm behind 0 will give you extra leverage. If you prefer spinning lower gears with a faster cadence, you'll do better closer to 0. Adjust the saddle accordingly.

4. **Saddle tilt.** Lay a yardstick along the length of the saddle to see its angle. Do this with the bike on a level surface (like the floor) with something horizontal in the background (like a windowsill) to compare to the yardstick. A level seat works well for the road, but for mountain biking, it is better to tip the nose down a degree or two. Be careful. A little downward tilt can reduce crotch pressure and make it easier to move back and forth, but too much will cause you to constantly slide forward and put excessive weight on your arms. Never angle the nose up. It will press harder into your crotch and snag your shorts when you go from standing to sitting.

5. **Foot position on the pedal.** Adjust each cleat fore/aft to put the ball of your foot directly above or as much as 5 millimeters in front of the pedal axle. (If the ball is behind the axle, you'll pedal on your toes and risk straining the muscles and tendons of your foot and calf.) If you're riding clipless pedals, look for a model that allows your feet to pivot, or float, a few degrees before releasing. This lets your feet assume their natural angle on the pedals. Your ankles and knees will thank you. Adjust the cleat angle so your heel has to travel the same distance left or right to reach the release point. Check this with your bike on a stationary

trainer. Pedal easily to let your feet find their natural position, then release to the inside and outside repeatedly. Keep adjusting until you have it right for both feet.

6. **Crankarm length.** In general, mountain bikers benefit from long levers. So for optimum pedaling power, all but the smallest riders (shorter than 5-foot-4) should use 175-mm crankarms rather than the 170-mm length commonly found on road bikes. Don't go longer than 175 mm unless you're a top NBA draft pick; that's because long crankarms will bash on the ground and send you sailing.

7. **Cockpit dimensions.** The key requirement in the driver compartment is to have enough room to move. When you're standing and the wheel is pointed straight ahead, make sure there is at least an inch of clearance between the handlebar grips and your knees when they're fully to the front. This lets you pedal while surging forward to get your wheel over an obstacle. If your knees come too close or even hit, you need more reach. Hopefully, you can make the correction with a longer stem and not have to swap the frame for one that has a longer top tube. Conversely, your handlebar must be close enough to let you extend your arms and push your buttocks all the way behind the saddle. You need this position for steep downhills and drop-offs.

8. **Handlebar and stem height.** Here's what to look for: When riding normally with slightly bent elbows, you should have roughly a 45-degree bend at the waist. From this position you can lower your chest for a more aero position at high speeds and to weight the front wheel for steering traction on climbs. But you also can raise your chest to lighten the front wheel over obstacles and increase weight on the rear wheel for climbing traction. Note, however, that many freeriders and downhillers prefer a more upright riding position, because (a) they don't do much climbing and (b) it gives them more control in rough terrain. Experiment and go with what feels best.

9. **Handlebar bend and width.** Most flat bars have a bend, or sweep, of 3 degrees; position the bar to give you the most natural angle for your wrists. Riser bars are being seen on all types of mountain bikes, not just on the downhill machines where they gained popularity. As opposed to traditional flat bars, risers have an upward bend and maybe 1 to 3 inches more width, making them substantially wider than your shoulders. They give you a more upright position, help you get your weight off the front wheel so you can loft it more easily, and slow your steering input slightly to increase stability.

10. **Bar end position.** If you use them, bar ends should be positioned so your wrists are straight (not cocked) while standing. This lets you apply maximum torque on out-of-saddle climbs, which is where bar ends are most useful.

11. **Brake lever position.** You tend to squeeze the levers hardest when standing, crouched above the bike on a steep descent. So that's the situation in which the levers need to be most accessible and comfortable. Rotate them so that in this riding position they give you straight (not cocked) wrists. If you set them for ideal access when you're in the saddle, your wrists will be at too sharp an angle when you stand.

Okay, you've carefully worked your way through all 11 position checks. You've ridden in a range of situations to test how well your position works. You've tweaked a couple of things. You've nailed it. Think you're done? Not quite.

There's one final step: You need to carefully record all the measurements and keep them in your training log, toolbox, or other safe place. Then, if you crash and knock things out of place or need to install new parts, you'll know exactly how to position them. You'll also have a much easier time setting up a loaner bike or even your next new one. Remember, your ideal position results from adjusting your bike to fit your body, not forcing your body to accommodate the bike. Once you're sitting pretty, record the numbers.

GLOSSARY

One final tip: Learn the lingo. This glossary will help you understand cycling's many special words and phrases when you're visiting bike shops or chatting with other riders. Though not every term is used in this book, you'll hear them all when you're involved in the sport.

A

Aerobic: Exercise at an intensity that allows the body's need for oxygen to be continually met. This intensity can be sustained for long periods.

Anaerobic: Exercise above the intensity at which the body's need for oxygen can be met. This intensity can be sustained only briefly.

Apex: The sharpest part of a turn where the transition from entering to exiting takes place.

B

Beginner: The NORBA category for novice recreational racers. A rider must advance to the Sport category after placing in the top five in five Beginner races.

Blow up: To suddenly be unable to continue at the required pace due to overexertion.

Bonk: To run out of energy, usually because the rider has failed to eat or drink enough.

Bunny-hop: A way to ride over obstacles such as rocks or logs in which both wheels leave the ground.

C

Cadence: The number of times during 1 minute that a foot completes a pedal stroke. Also called pedal rpm.

Chain slap: When the chain bangs against the frame's right chainstay (the tube between the rear dropout and the bottom bracket).

Chainring: A sprocket on the crankset. Includes the big, middle, and small (granny). Short version is "ring."

Chainsuck: When the chain sticks to the chainring teeth during a downshift and gets drawn up and jammed between the small ring and the frame.

Clean: To ride a tough section without dabbing.

Clydesdale: A large rider. At some cross-country races, there is a Clydesdale class for riders who weigh more than 200 pounds.

Cog: A sprocket on the rear wheel's cassette or freewheel.

Compression: The act of a shock while absorbing a bump.

Compression damping: An adjustment that allows the rider to determine how a shock reacts to bump forces.

Contact patch: The portion of a tire in touch with the ground.

Countersteer: To briefly turn the handlebar in the opposite direction you want to go, helping initiate a lean in the desired direction.

Cross-country: The traditional and most popular type of mountain bike race. Most courses mix fire road with singletrack. Races may be point to point, one long loop, or two or more laps of a shorter loop.

Cross training: Combining sports for mental refreshment and physical conditioning, especially during cycling's off season.

Cyclocross: An off-road event in which the course has obstacles that force riders to dismount and run with their bikes.

D

Dab: To put a foot on the ground to prevent falling over.

Damping: Determines the rate of compression and rebound in a front or rear suspension. On most suspensions, damping is adjustable, letting you set the shock so that it returns to its original position in time for the next bump but doesn't recoil so fast that it makes the bike bounce.

Doubletrack: Two parallel trails formed by the wheel ruts of off-road vehicles. Also called a Jeep trail.

Downhill: A race held at ski areas. The fastest rider from top to bottom wins. Competitors wear protective clothes and pads ("body armor") and usually ride special dual-suspension bikes designed for maximum shock absorption.

Downshift: To shift to a lower gear (a larger cog or smaller chainring).

Drift: When inertia or centrifugal force pulls the bike offline, often in a turn. Also called wheel drift.

Dual slalom: As in skiing, riders race downhill between gates on parallel courses. Unlike in a downhill race, in which the clock determines the winner, dual slalom is head-to-head elimination. Riders continue advancing until they lose.

Dualie: A bike with front and rear suspension. Short for "dual suspension."

E

Elastomer: A compressible, rubberlike material used to absorb shock in some suspension systems.

Endo: To crash by going over the bike's handlebar. Short for "end over end."

Expert: The NORBA category between Sport and Semi-Pro. It's for riders who have developed advanced racing skill, strength, and stamina. Riders can remain Expert for as long as they wish.

F

Fire road: A dirt or gravel road in the backcountry wide enough to allow access by emergency vehicles.

Freeride: A gonzo riding style that encompasses steep drops, jumps, and often, man-made obstacles

G

Glutes: The gluteal muscles of the buttocks. They are key to pedaling power.

Glycogen: A fuel derived as glucose (sugar) from carbohydrate and stored in the muscles and liver. It's the primary energy source for high-intensity riding. Reserves are normally depleted after about 2½ hours of riding.

Granny gear: The lowest gear ratio, combining the small chainring with the largest cassette cog. It's mainly used for very steep climbs.

Granny ring: The smallest of the three chainrings.

H

Hamstrings: The muscles on the back of the thighs; not well developed by cycling.

Hardtail: A bike with no rear suspension.

I

IMBA: International Mountain Bicycling Association, an organization dedicated to protecting and expanding trail access for mountain bikers. Address: P.O. Box 7578, Boulder, CO 80306; 303-545-9011; www.imba.com.

Interval training: A type of workout in which periods of intense effort are alternated with periods of easy effort for recovery.

J

Jam: A period of hard, fast riding.

Jump: A quick, hard acceleration.

L

Lactate threshold (LT): The exertion level at which the body can no longer produce energy aerobically, resulting in the buildup of lactic acid. This is marked by muscle fatigue, pain, and shallow, rapid breathing. The heart rate at which this occurs is called lactate threshold heart rate (LTHR). Also called anaerobic threshold.

Lactic acid: A substance formed during anaerobic metabolism when there is incomplete breakdown of glucose. It rapidly produces muscle fatigue and pain.

Ladder bridge: An elevated, man-made structure that demands tremendous balance and concentration to ride.

M

Max VO$_2$: The maximum amount of oxygen that can be consumed during all-out exertion. This is a key indicator of a person's potential in cycling and other aerobic sports. It's largely genetically determined but can be improved somewhat by training.

Modulate: The progressive action of braking. Brakes that feel smooth and progressively powerful are known to have good "modulation."

N

NORBA: National Off-Road Bicycle Association, the division of USA Cycling that governs mountain bike racing. Address: One Olympic Plaza, Colorado Springs, CO 80909; 719-866-4581; www.usacycling.org.

Nose wheelie: Opposite of a wheelie.

O

Observed trials: A slow-speed event in which the objective is to ride a difficult, obstacle-filled course without putting a foot down. The rider with the fewest dabs wins. Also called simply trials.

Off the back: Describes one or more riders who have failed to keep pace with the main group. Also referred to as OTB.

P

Pedal rpm: See Cadence.

Pinch flat: An internal puncture caused by the tube being squeezed against the rim. It results from riding into an object too hard and makes two small holes. Also called a snakebite.

Preload: The adjustable spring tension in a suspension fork or rear shock. It determines how far the suspension compresses under body weight and how much travel remains to absorb impacts.

Presta: The narrow European-style valve found on some inner tubes. A small metal cap on its end must be unscrewed for air to enter or exit.

Pro: NORBA's top racing category. Most professional racers are sponsored and travel the world to compete in major events.

Quadriceps: The muscle group on the front of the thigh; well developed by cycling.

Rebound: The act of a shock springing back from a bump.

Rebound damping: An adjustment that allows the rider to determine how quickly a shock springs back from bump forces.

Ring: See Chainring.

Schrader: An inner tube valve identical to those found on car tires. A tiny plunger in the center of its opening must be depressed for air to enter or exit.

Semi-Pro: The NORBA category (also known as Elite) between Expert and Pro. It serves as a stepping-stone for riders who aspire to race professionally as well as a way for pro teams to identify new talent.

Singletrack: A trail so narrow that two cyclists can't easily ride side by side, which makes passing difficult or impossible.

Spinning: Pedaling with a relatively fast cadence using small to moderate gears.

Sport: The NORBA category between Beginner and Expert. It's usually the largest field at any race. After finishing in the top five in five races, a Sport rider must advance to Expert.

Switchback: A turn greater than 90 degrees. Switchbacks are found mainly on hills that are too steep to be ascended (or descended) using a direct path.

T

Trackstand: A skill where a rider comes to a full stop without putting a foot down. On a technical trail, a trackstand lets you pause to decide what to do next, and it may save you from toppling over if you suddenly come to an unexpected halt.

Travel: The maximum distance a suspension fork or rear shock can compress.

Trials: See Observed trials.

U

Upshift: To shift to a higher gear (a smaller cog or larger chainring).

W

Wheelie: To elevate the front wheel and ride on the rear wheel only. The opposite is called a nose wheelie.

INDEX

Boldface page references indicate photographs and illustrations.